THE 90% SOLUTION

HIGHER RETURNS, LESS RISK

DAVID ROGERS

WILEY

John Wiley & Sons, Inc.

Published by John Wiley & Sons, Inc., Hoboken, New Jersey.
Published simultaneously in Canada.

Charts or data produced by TeleChart 2005® which is a registered trademark of Worden
Brothers, Inc., Five Oaks Office Park, 4905 Pine Cone Drive, Durham, NC 27707.
Phone: 800-776-4940 or 919-408-0542. www.Worden.com.

For general information on our other products and services or for technical support,
please contact our Customer Care Department within the United States at (800) 762-2974,
outside the United States at (317) 572-3993 or fax (317) 572-4002.

Wiley also publishes its books in a variety of electronic formats. Some content that appears
in print may not be available in electronic books. For more information about Wiley
products, visit our web site at www.wiley.com.

Library of Congress Cataloging-in-Publication Data:
Rogers, David, 1951 May 7–
  The 90% solution : higher returns, less risk / David Rogers.
    p. cm.
  Includes index.
  ISBN-13: 978-0-471-77081-7 (cloth)
  ISBN-10: 0-471-77081-7 (cloth)
  1. Portfolio management. 2. Investments. I. Title. II. Title: Ninety
percent solution.
  HG4529.5.R64 2006
  332.6—dc22

                                          2006011071

Printed in the United States of America.

10 9 8 7 6 5 4 3 2 1

This book is dedicated to

my parents, Pete and Zelma,

and

Ben Bird, June Gaede, and Florence Gholz,
who taught me thought, creativity, and expression.

Contents

Act V   Other Approaches   203

Acknowledgments

Writing a first book is surely a labor of love—until you discover what you've gotten yourself into.

No written work of any consequence is brought to life in a vacuum. From our earliest days, we are influenced by people, places, and events. Some of them have an immediately obvious impact on our lives and our thinking. Others' impact will not be known or appreciated until years later, if at all.

I would be remiss if I didn't first acknowledge the people in my life who have rarely told me "no," and have been quick to pick me up for salvage when I fell down or embarrassed myself. My parents, Pete and Zelma Rogers, have not always understood my ambitions, but they have always supported me in my endeavors. Their love is only exceeded by God's love for each of us, one and all, and His forgiveness for our shortcomings as we try to find our way.

Ben Bird, Florence Gholz, and June Gaede, to whom I have also dedicated this book, were elementary and secondary school teachers in Bakersfield, California. Each of them had a profound impact, not just on my early academic training, but on how I perceived the world. So many times we are guilty of going on in life from our humble beginnings, hopefully climbing a ladder to some measure of accomplishment, fame, or notoriety—but many of us fail to look back and acknowledge those who gave us a helping hand, even guided us, up those first critical steps.

Frank Falero was also a teacher with a profound impact, an economics professor at California State University, Bakersfield, where I finished my college degree after stints at the University of Redlands and Claremont McKenna College. In 1977, Frank selected me for CSUB's entry in the graduate-level competition of the International Collegiate Business Policy Games. In doing so, he set me on a course for discovering business, economics, and the markets from which I have yet to look back.

I also want to thank my friend Ken Erbeznik, who in the mid-1990s doggedly pressed me to write a book. Well, here it is, Ken, if 11 years later than you expected. Thanks for your encouragement, and I hope it lives up to your expectations.

Jack Norberg has been one of my most constructively critical editors off and on for 11 years. The President of Standard Investment Chartered, Inc., in Costa Mesa, California, in my research report writing Jack has torn apart my past participles, compound and complicated sentences, and use of passive tense, always encouraging me to maintain a high level of creative expression with punchier, get-to-the-point messaging. He challenges me to tell a better story, more efficiently. Beyond that, Jack has been a valued mentor. For his friendship and support I am deeply indebted.

You will read some about Jeff Heisler in other parts of this book. My longtime friend has helped me avoid complete embarrassment among academia, more than once. Where academic works could be useful in support of my basic thesis, Jeff made some valuable suggestions.

Richard Bryant is President of Capital Investment Companies, of Raleigh, North Carolina. He helped me lay the foundation for what evolved as my mutual fund asset allocation services. His support and influence must be recognized. Our business relationship was rendered obsolete by some of the very forces described in this book, but I trust our friendship will endure.

Roger Reynolds, a former colleague of mine at Marion Bass Securities in Charlotte, North Carolina; and Mark Collinson, a partner at CCG Investor Relations in Los Angeles, have been kind enough to proofread substantial portions of this text for readability, grammar, and accuracy.

Several practicing money managers in various cities around the globe served as sounding boards from time to time in writing this book. I have learned that most professional managers value their privacy and relative obscurity, so I will not mention them by name or firm. You know who you are, and I thank you. Geographically, they are from a wide range of cities and towns, including New York, Boston, Los Angeles, San Francisco, Portland, Seattle, Chicago, Denver, Dallas, San Diego, Charlotte, Atlanta, Blowing Rock, Newport Beach, London, Paris, Frankfurt, and Taiwan.

Through the years, I have made many friends in the industry among colleagues and clients. Many have had a special impact or influence on my career development, including Ed Barys, Tom Andersen, Dwayne Wee, Francis Moore, Wendell Mew, John Robinson, Leo Himmelblau, Jack Frager, Dick Vance, Larry Oakford, Jim Tompkins, Jim Mulka, Richard DeMartini, Chuck Howard, Ed Trevillian, Ben Brooks, Emil Skocpol, Ben

Murillo, Kent Williams, Craig Weston, Craig Pieringer, Will Hickey, Binkley Shorts, Lloyd Culbertson, Michael Michaud, Ron Johnston, Jeff Fox, Andy Neely, Ron Kruszewski, Paul Ligon, Jack McDermott, Bill Schmidt, Otis Bradley, Doyle Holmes, Marion Bass, and Bill Ferry, among many others. Your friendship and counsel are appreciated.

Finally, but definitely not least, I am indebted to my friend and mentor Lee Glasner, the now retired senior executive of Financial Relations Board and winner of numerous annual report writing awards when he was active in the financial public relations arena. Thankfully, Lee proofread every word and graphic of this book for substance, grammar, and style—but now I am having nightmares with red lines throughout every report, editorial, or book I have ever written or intend to write!

Debra Englander is my Executive Editor at John Wiley & Sons, Inc. Her contributions have been invaluable, as she and her team (including Greg Friedman, Todd Tedesco, and Shelley Flannery) have pushed me toward better definition of my theme and a more logical progression of thought. Their patience with a first-time author is greatly appreciated, but may also qualify Debra for martyrdom.

I am so deeply indebted to my best friend, life partner, and wife, Kim Jenkins Rogers. She is my Valentine and my most trusted confidante, with whom I share life's secrets, mysteries, and adventures.

Thanks to all of the people who have helped shape my thinking about the markets and investing, whether you knew it at the time or not. And thanks to that special breed of investor: the one clamoring for superior results, not willing to settle for mediocrity. This book is really for you, and nobody else.

Introduction

The number crunchers who analyze investments for a living will tell you that investment performance is generally explained in two segments. First, there is the "beta" portion, then the "alpha" portion.

Beta is passive, because neither you nor your manager has to do anything. If you are invested in stocks, then beta says that a good chunk of your performance is due to overall stock market trends. It's that part of portfolio performance that is improving because stock valuations are improving, generally.

Alpha is active. It represents how much you or your portfolio manager's decision-making skills make a difference to the investment results. A positive alpha is every portfolio manager's bliss. A persistently negative alpha may be his worst nightmare, because he'll have to hire more talented salespeople to sell his underperforming services. If he earns a positive alpha, filling his pride and pockets, then the accounts or mutual funds he manages have outperformed the broader stock market relative to the risk he took.

Alpha was conjured up by people who participate in and analyze the investing process. Intuitively, their invention of alpha implies one very simple truth: The single most important factor in the performance of *any* well-diversified stock portfolio will most likely be discovered as the concurrent direction of the overall stock market. In fact, you will learn in these pages that if you "get the market right" you may have done as much as 90% or more of the portfolio manager's job. This is true, and not just in up markets. You will also see that getting the market right allows you to more effectively counter the potential adverse consequences of the market's corrective phases—*if* you have a plan and one or more strategies to take advantage.

The 90% Solution: It is about understanding this important but largely neglected concept, and some practical ways to take advantage.

Some of my thoughts will be seen as common sense. A few may be controversial. As you will see in Chapter 1, over a period of many years the financial services industry drifted toward merchandising its wares and away from the general market's importance to returns. By understanding and using the overall market's power and influence, an investor can *capitalize* on the market and simplify his investment life. He gets his investment costs under control. At the very least, he can neutralize the potential adverse impact on his stock portfolio when the market is in a corrective phase.

Perhaps he will even profit from a market decline. If he gets a little adventurous, the investor might even *enhance profits in up markets with only marginal assumption of additional risk*. Enhance returns; better manage risk—*The 90% Solution* is about *not being satisfied with mediocrity*. Sadly, most of the investment industry today seeks only mediocre returns, even if still asking for premium compensation.

NO BONES ABOUT IT

In July 2005, I met an orthopedic surgeon in Charlotte, North Carolina. As we became acquainted, he shared with me that he had a sizable stock portfolio. In turn, I disclosed that I had just agreed to write a book about the importance of the overall stock market's direction on the performance of *any well-diversified equity portfolio.*

After just a moment's hesitation he replied, "Well, I only invest in *good* companies. In fact, I buy the absolute best I can find for their long-term prospects. They either have high, increasing dividend payments, or good potential for share price appreciation. All I can say about your book's premise is that when the Standard & Poor's 500 Stock Index collapsed between March 2000 and November 2002, the share values of my so-called 'good companies' got absolutely crushed."

That's why I am writing this book. The vast majority of investors in the United States were taught to invest the very same way: Buy shares of a company you believe has good long-term business potential. Better yet, diversify your risk and invest in several companies (in several different industries), each with excellent potential to increase its dividend or appreciate in share value. Then hold on to your stocks (and maybe pray a little) through every market environment: up, down, or sideways.

Like so many investors during the first years of this new millennium, my doctor friend might benefit from a different approach. Surely, these investors ask, there must be a way to earn superior investment returns while more effectively managing the risks and costs inherent to stock market investing.

In fact, most investors would benefit from rethinking their investing strategy. Just because we have bought into the concepts, products, and services the financial services industry is selling, does that mean it is right for us now? Times and the markets have changed. Investors as well as sales organizations, management companies, and regulatory authorities must wake up, shake loose the cobwebs, and explore anew their long and short-term investment strategies—or be stuck in the throes of mediocrity or, even worse, sub-par performance.

I don't have all the answers. No one does. My objective in writing this book is that it be a "thinking springboard" for the reader, whether investor, broker, salesperson, money manager, or regulator. Every investor, every stock market participant, needs to find an investment strategy to match his or her comfort level of market understanding, risk tolerance, and resources—indeed, to find his or her *investment personality*.

If you are a mutual fund investor, you will probably look at your investments differently after reading this book. I am critical of many industry players because they are unwitting pawns of the game. Most of the issues I raise show how we have collectively drifted away from certain truths about the investing mission. We simply have not adapted the playing field and the rules of the game to the new market realities—and certainly today we have an abundance of new opportunities.

Somewhere, somehow, somebody convinced influential people that the market was "efficient," that the prices were "always right," and that market direction is unpredictable and cannot be harnessed. That idea took hold and became gospel according to adherents of buy-and-hold and traditional active management, as well as a wide assortment of indexing and asset allocation professionals.

Don't get me wrong. Predicting the overall market's direction over time is no small and painless undertaking. In fact, *predicting* market direction is a nonsensical endeavor. The critics of market timing have it right. Predicting market direction consistently is impossible.

But, based on the identification of historically observed market patterns and business or economic circumstance, what if you could accurately establish the *probability* of future market direction 60% of the time? How about 70%? Or 80%?

In fact, there are ways to establish (and take advantage of) the *probable* market direction and market conditions. They allow you to enhance returns and more effectively manage risk-and do so in more cost-effective ways than other investors today are utilizing. There are ways to put the number-1 explainer of portfolio performance to work *for* you, rather than allowing it to work against you.

If you are a mutual fund portfolio manager, traditional investment advisor, or conventional asset allocation adherent, after reading this book you may come away with a new appreciation for your role in the investment process and maybe a new openness to looking at things differently. New ways to chase that elusive *alpha* will register. You might even quit your job and start a hedge fund because you will know that mutual fund management as we have known it is a dying profession. Traditional, long-only fund managers are, increasingly, unable to compete in the new managed money marketplace that is already materializing. Some of the changes are subtle, others profound, but the symptoms of change a-comin' are there. They are likely to take years of evolution, but maybe fewer than you might hope.

If you are an individual investor managing your own equity portfolio, or a hedge fund manager unencumbered by the restraints of the typical mutual fund charter or investment advisor mission statement, then you may be prompted to rethink or expand your strategies. To coin a phrase, this is not your grandfather's stock market.

ACT I

SLAYING THE DRAGONS

In *The Fountainhead*, Ayn Rand presents an exalted view of mankind's creative potential. Her story centers on an architect who dares to challenge the Establishment. She celebrates her hero's rejection of doing things the way they have always been done; his uncompromising stands in favor of truth, honesty, and creativity; and his general dissatisfaction with ambitions aimed at only achieving mediocrity.

These themes came to mind as I was having coffee and reading the morning paper recently at the Higher Grounds coffee shop in Boone, North Carolina. Engaging me in conversation, Matt Scott, the owner, had an interesting observation. He said, "David, as a small investor, sometimes I feel like I'm part of a herd of sheep being led to slaughter. There are so many investment choices, so many different kinds of mutual funds, so many different brokerage firms, so many different media identifying themselves as stock market research. But the truth is they all seem to be so similar and so wholly inadequate when it comes to achieving superior investment performance. Why do most so-called professional efforts in the stock market seem to be pursuing only mediocre investment results?"

At its core, Act I ("Slaying the Dragons") is intended to help answer this question: Where and how did the financial services industry wander away from the pursuit of superior investment results?

1

Lessons from Shakespeare's Bastard Son

Investment returns from the stocks of *successful* companies generally *outpace the rate of inflation over the long-term.* Armed with this knowledge, and examples like General Electric, Microsoft, Boeing, Cisco Systems, Intel, and a host of other well-established "blue chips," the financial services industry has done two things especially well in the last 30 years:

1. It has sold John Q. Public on the virtues of *stock market investing as a wealth accumulation strategy.*
2. It has also sold Mr. Public on the concept of *professional capital management (especially mutual funds) as the best way to accumulate wealth.*

From the infancy of professional management, the majority of portfolio managers have been what are termed "active managers." Although my academic friends tell me that rudimentary futures and options contracts date back to the ancient Greeks, derivatives probably weren't even a figment of Graham and Dodd's imagination. No one knew about "indexing" or "passive investing" in the early years of money management.

For those new to the stock market, Benjamin Graham and David Dodd authored the classic bible of "value investing," *Security Analysis*. First published in 1934 by McGraw-Hill, it remains an enduring foundation for the investment styles of many active portfolio managers.

My mission in this book is not to detract from Graham and Dodd's gospel, because it is exceptional work. Nor is my mission to dispute any other portfolio manager's style or stock selection method. *My mission is simply to help people harness the power of the single most important factor in diversified portfolio performance: the overall market.* Don't ignore its importance. Rather, *use its influence* in new, better, and more cost-effective ways.

Classically defined as someone who does a better job than the next guy of finding and owning stocks, the "pure" active manager is 100% "long" stocks—all of the time—even if he periodically repositions his capital (by repositioning, he sells one or more stocks, for whatever reason, and reinvests the capital in other equities).

The best analogy I can think of is that he is in a "team" horse race that never ends. He is going to win the race, he claims, because of the "horses," or stocks, he selects to run the race. His advantage is being able to pull a replacement horse out of the corral during the race when one of his other worthy steeds grows tired or simply proves himself unworthy.

For most portfolio managers, having 4% of assets on the sidelines is considered a high cash position. The portfolio manager's job, as it has evolved, is to be as fully invested as possible in *equity* investment opportunities. That's what his clients demand, because conceptually that is what they have grown to understand: Invest in, or "own," good companies.

From inception, active managers advertised themselves as able to earn far superior returns relative to mere amateurs because of their "stock pickin'" abilities. They are "security selectors," as David Swenson, Yale University's chief investment officer, described them in *Unconventional Success* (Free Press, Simon & Schuster, 2005), excerpted in the July 2005 issue of *Institutional Investor*. They aim to be above average "... in a brutally competitive atmosphere. Surrounded by highly qualified, highly motivated, highly compensated competitors, the active manager struggles to identify and exploit an edge that leads to superior results." Acknowledges Swenson, "Many try, but few succeed in winning the active management game."

Why don't *more* traditional professional advisors win the active management game? Why do *the vast majority* post performance records that are best characterized as only mediocre?

My answer is that it's about *competition and delusion*, as well as the structure of the game itself. It's also about what the financial services industry and even business schools have taught America as the best way to invest in the stock market.

WOW, WHAT A GOOD BUSINESS MODEL!

For their skill in constructing portfolios, traditional investment managers are paid a fee. As it evolved (and was endorsed by government regulators), the fee is based on the dollars of assets under management.

It's *not a bad business model*, with equal parts incentive to (1) earn profits (performance), (2) add new money to manage (marketing), and (3) protect capital (risk management). And once there are sufficient assets to cover overhead, the majority of fees from new assets under management drop straight to the firm's profits. Add a trader here, a research analyst there, some accounting staff, and maybe a couple of customer service or sales reps, but many managers can supervise the investment of *$1 billion* with only marginally more overhead than that with which they managed *$100 million*.

Of course, all good business models invite competition. As professional money management gained acceptance, the investment marketplace experienced what a Marketing 101 student learns as "product differentiation." Faced with competition, active managers were not just better stock pickers, but suddenly they were "value managers," or "growth managers," or "equity income managers." Maybe they became "small cap managers," "mid-cap managers," or "large cap managers." Or they were "momentum managers," "growth-at-a-reasonable-price managers," "conservative growth managers," "core growth managers"—and so on.

Professional portfolio managers distinguish themselves by their investment style, or risk orientation, or stock selection method. And, of course, *their* style, *their* orientation, *their* method, and *their* discipline are, without question, the keys to investment performance—or so they advertise.

Somewhere, somehow, professional portfolio management, the American investment industry, and investors as a whole got sidetracked, like Shakespeare's self-proclaimed bastard son: Sir William D'Avenant. An English poet and playwright in the 1600s, D'Avenant was most famous for attempting to rewrite his renowned father's plays. He even tried to give *Romeo & Juliet* a happy ending!

Professional money managers have rewritten history to serve their own interests, too, albeit with innocent or perhaps naïve intentions. Each manager has a different investment style or stock selection method that, he claims, distinguishes him from his peers. Yet every single one aspires to results that are above average when compared to a performance benchmark. Most often it is an "overall" stock market average, like the Standard & Poor's (S&P) 500 Stock Index.

When it comes to investment performance, the sad reality is that most active managers are closer to being the same, than unique. And most underperform their benchmarks. Why is this true?

The mainstream of investing Americana (and this includes professional and nonprofessional investors alike) are traditional. They don't run hedge funds or commodity pools. They don't supervise mutual fund allocation strategies. And most certainly they do not engage in market timing. And they are *not* into indexing.

They are active managers running mutual fund, insurance, or pension portfolios. Maybe they are investment advisors managing the typical, well-diversified "long-only" stock portfolios of affluent individuals. Maybe they are affluent individuals looking after their own portfolios.

What are their obstacles to earning truly superior investment returns? They are: (1) *only* buying good companies, and (2) *over*emphasizing diversification.

Investors are only buying good companies. In my years as a research analyst and institutional salesman, I had the privilege to meet some of the smartest and most successful institutional money managers in the business. Many were educated at the finest business schools in the country. A number evolved in their careers from other industry disciplines, maybe from brokerage firm research, trading, or sales positions. A few had roots in academia and were highly successful individual investors, so becoming a registered investment advisor was a natural career development. One fellow even won a newspaper-sponsored, stock-picking contest a few years back, and leveraged that into a professional investment advisory career.

In no way do I mean to denigrate the skill or importance of traditional portfolio managers. Obviously, you don't want them picking the stocks of companies that go bankrupt in six months! Constructing portfolios by selecting individual stocks *is* important—it just may not be *as* important as they would like you to believe.

The vast majority of these managers share a common value, if not mandate, with my Charlotte-based orthopedic surgeon: "I only invest in good companies." I've heard this mantra many times. Each one of these very bright men and women assert that the most important factor in their investment performance is the *way* they pick their good companies, or in other words, *their* investment style, *their* research, and *their* stock selection methods. So is this true?

TRUTH BE TOLD

While it may very well be true regarding the individual stock selections they make, in reality they are trying to rewrite the truth with such claims when it comes to their well-diversified portfolios, much like Shakespeare's bastard son trying to rewrite *Romeo & Juliet* with a happy ending. Usually unspoken by them all is that the single most important factor in *diversified* portfolio performance has nothing to do with style, orientation, research, or the security selection method. My orthopedic surgeon friend knows the truth intuitively, and by experience: *The single most important factor in the performance of any well-diversified stock portfolio is the concurrent performance of the overall stock market.*

Stock selection method doesn't matter. Investment style doesn't matter, nor does the average size of the companies comprising the portfolios or the expense ratio. And it doesn't matter whether a mutual fund is "load" or "no load," or whether the portfolio is managed by an individual, man or woman, team, or committee. All that stuff is trivial compared to the *impact of stock market direction on a well-diversified portfolio's performance.*

Don't just take my word for it. There are numerous academic studies by professors at some of the nation's finest business schools, each asserting that the performance of the asset class (i.e., stocks vs. bonds) represents as much as, if not more than 90% of a well-diversified portfolio's performance.

Academic studies aside, the proof is commonly quantified. In the 1980s, "performance analytics" gained significant traction in the investment marketplace. Its practitioners found statistical methods to slice and dice the performance of any mutual fund or investment portfolio for which data was available, including what became popularly known as Modern Portfolio Theory (MPT).

Among the tools developed is a statistic called "R-Squared." Generated by regression analysis, R-Squared is the degree of variation in the return on a stock portfolio that is accounted for by the variation in the overall stock market. Restated, R-Squared answers the question of how much of a portfolio's performance is explained by the overall market, most often represented by the S&P 500 Stock Index—the amount of performance that would have been earned with or without the portfolio manager's skill or intervention.

As you might expect, the R-Squared of an index fund constructed to replicate the S&P 500 will be 100% if the benchmark used as the independent variable *is* the S&P 500. But, for now, let's ignore the indexers. The traditional, long-only equity mutual fund is an acceptable surrogate for almost any well-diversified, long-only portfolio that might be constructed. Look at these, and you will understand my claim about the market's importance to portfolio performance regardless of investment style, research, or selection method.

Morningstar, Inc. (NASDAQ Symbol: MORN) is a popular, Chicago-based mutual fund rating service (www.morningstar.com). It publishes a variety of MPT statistics on every stock or bond mutual fund for which data is retrievable. Yahoo! Finance lists 8,434 U.S. equity funds alone in its Morningstar-derived database as this book is being written. Morningstar publishes an R-Squared statistic for each equity fund versus the Standard & Poor's 500, which is commonly accepted as best representing the overall market. They also publish an R-Squared for each fund versus a "best fit" index, but we are going to focus on the S&P 500 as the most commonly accepted benchmark for the overall stock market.

When I first looked at R-Squared versus the S&P 500, I speculated that the Five-Star funds in Morningstar's universe would most likely demonstrate that a portfolio manager's investment style or method is the most important factor in performance. Five-Star funds are so designated because of their superior historical returns relative to the risks assumed over the most recent 36 months, so it's a *backward-looking assessment*.

As much as you might wish it to be true, a Morningstar rating doesn't tell you how these funds are going to do in the future. They only evaluate and report on the way the funds have performed historically, whether a Five-Star fund or a One-Star fund. Nonetheless, there is an implicit suggestion among financial services salespeople that once a five-star fund, always a five-star fund. Yes, the five-star performers have been stellar the past three years and certainly merit priority consideration, but you have to dig deeper than that to ascertain whether or not their above-average performance and risk management might be sustainable.

I gathered R-Squared data on all of the Five-Star equity funds in each of the different investment styles categorized by Morningstar: Large Cap Value; Large Cap Growth; Large Cap Blend; Mid-Cap Value; Mid-Cap Growth; Mid-Cap Blend; Small Cap Value; Small Cap Growth; and Small Cap Blend. Surely, I postulated, the great preponderance of Five-Star performers in each category would stand out because of their managers' unique abilities.

I found the opposite to be true. A low R-Squared among all Five-Star funds was 70%. A *very low* R-Squared was 50%. In all but a scant few exceptions, at least 50% of Five-Star funds' respective performances are explained: *not* by a manager's superior research, *not* by a manager's gender, *not* by whether the manager was a team, committee, or an individual, *not* by the type of stocks that were bought, and *not* by the manager's "stock pickin'" skill. No! With scant few exceptions, at least 50% of Five-Star fund performance was explained by the *concurrent performance of the S&P 500*—according to commonly accepted principles of statistical regression analysis, MPT and R-Squared. Where else can someone get paid premium compensation while having someone or something else do the lion's share of their job?

In fact, the more popular a fund is (the more assets under management), or the greater the number of stocks in the portfolio, or the larger the average market capitalization of the companies bought for the portfolio— the more likely it is that its R-Squared will approach 100%.

In Tables 1.1 through 1.7, I have included the R-Squared results for all of the funds designated as Five-Star small cap and large cap performers by Morningstar on February 18, 2006 (intuitively, mid-cap funds fall somewhere in between the performance ratings of the small-cap and large-cap funds). Look at these throughout the year and the names in the backward-looking assessment comprising the five-star roster may change, but the R-Squared performance rankings of the top-tier performers rarely change to any great degree. I went through this same exercise in August, October, and December 2005, and the results were all very similar. *Most* of the R-Squared results for traditional, long-only stock funds are between 60 and 99%, whether they are top performers or bottom feeders.

TABLE 1.1 R-Squared versus S&P 500, Five-Star **Large Cap Blend** Funds, as of February 18, 2006

Fund	3-Yr. R-Squared	3-Yr. Alpha	Annual Turnover
Accessor Aggressive	93	2.95	4%
American Century Strat. Alloc.	90	2.67	171%
CMG Strategic Equity	90	3.44	64%
Cambiar Opportunity	84	1.64	43%
Exeter Equity	74	4.63	57%
Exeter Pro-Blend Maximum	76	3.96	61%
Exeter Tax Managed	75	3.79	68%
FMI Large Cap	75	5.52	40%
Fidelity Export & Multinational	89	4.54	68%
Gartmore Nationwide Leaders	63	3.79	N/A
Goldman Sachs Growth Strat.	84	6.52	44%
Hartford Capital Appreciation	84	5.49	93%
Janus Advisor Core Equity	78	4.21	80%
Janus Risk Managed Core	88	4.86	80%
Janus Contrarian	70	9.69	42%
Janus Core Equity	78	4.90	74%
Jennison 20/20 Focus	78	5.68	76%
Kobren Growth	89	3.04	30%
Longleaf Partners	79	0.26	13%
MDT All Cap Core	79	4.34	204%
Mairs & Power Growth	82	2.86	3%
Marathon Value	87	2.93	38%
Mass Mutual Select Focused	85	0.22	32%
Merrill Lynch Large Cap Core	66	5.40	94%
Morgan Stanley Equally Wt. S&P	93	2.13	14%
Neuberger Berman Partners	77	5.91	61%
Neuberger Berman Socially Responsible	80	2.54	21%
Old Mutual Analytic Defensive Equity	56	6.83	120%
Oppenheimer Main Street Opportunity	90	3.22	107%
Penn Street Adv. Sector Rotational	75	6.04	107%

TABLE 1.1   *(Continued)*

Fund	3-Yr. R-Squared	3-Yr. Alpha	Annual Turnover
Purisima Total Return	88	0.97	17%
Quaker Strategic Growth	64	7.97	205%
Russell LifePoints Eq. Agg.	92	4.55	3%
Rydex Nova C	99	−2.61	388%
Rydex Sector Rotation C	66	1.96	262%
Salomon Brothers Capital	78	3.02	131%
T. Rowe Price Personal Strat. Growth	95	3.38	52%
TCW Galileo Equities	86	2.17	32%
TCW Galileo Focused Equities	78	3.06	43%
Tocqueville	78	3.71	45%
Vanguard Primecap	85	4.39	12%

Rydex Nova is actually a leveraged index fund tied to the S&P 500, which accounts for its 99% R-Squared. Not a single R-Squared rating in this list of 41 Five-Star large cap "blend" funds is below 63. The average R-Squared for this group is 80.88%, meaning that the concurrent performance of the S&P 500 (or overall market) explains almost 81% of their performance. The level of portfolio turnover does not seem to make much of a difference in R-Squared, nor does it seem to have a large impact on alpha.

Source: Data from Morningstar, Inc.

Put in perspective, even in "high performance" Five-Star funds the overall market direction does from 60 to more than 90% of the portfolio manager's job.

But one of the most astounding observations I made when looking at Morningstar's performance data is that despite this, *America has bought into the investment industry's marketing mantra hook, line, and sinker.* Just look at the R-Squared results for the 25 largest U.S. equity funds in Table 1.7. In 7 out of the top 10 largest funds, and in 20 of the largest 25, *the overall stock market accounted for more than 80% of these managers' performance.*

TABLE 1.2   R-Squared versus S&P 500, Five-Star **Large Cap Growth** Funds, as of February 18, 2006

Fund	3-Yr. R-Squared	3-Yr. Alpha	Annual Turnover
ABM/AMRO Verdeus Select Growth	70	2.16	202%
AIM Multi-Sector	82	4.03	63%
AXA Enterprise Capital Appreciation	76	2.15	69%
Allianz CCM Capital Appreciation	78	1.88	137%
Amana Mutual Funds Trust Growth	76	9.64	2%
American Funds Amcap	88	0.56	16%
American Funds Growth Fund of America	88	3.47	20%
American Funds New Economy	87	0.73	32%
Bishop Street Strategic Growth	70	2.64	59%
Calvert Large Cap Growth	71	4.42	61%
Chase Growth	54	3.77	87%
Columbia Marisco 21st Century	72	5.50	130%
Dreyfus Premier Alpha Growth	64	0.99	88%
FMI Provident Trust Strategy	53	8.74	38%
Fidelity Capital Appreciation	79	3.54	109%
Fidelity Contrafund	72	7.69	64%
Fidelity Fifty	80	−4.53	110%
Fidelity Select Leisure	77	1.39	117%
Gartmore Inv. Destinations Aggr.	93	3.19	7%
Gartmore Inv. Destinations Mod. Aggr.	93	2.55	6%
Gartmore U.S. Growth Leaders	79	2.25	442%
Generation Wave Growth	83	3.14	40%
ING Partners Salomon Bros Aggr.	78	1.68	3%
Janus Advisor Forty	65	4.48	45%
Janus Advisor Growth & Income	77	2.65	43%
MFS Aggressive Growth Allocation	91	2.61	1%
Markman Total Return	72	2.14	472%
Marisco 21st Century	72	5.38	175%
Oppenheimer Enterprise	67	1.59	123%
Smith Barney Aggressive Growth	73	2.63	2%
TA IDEX Jennison Growth	84	−0.10	86%
TA IDEX Transamerica Equity	72	5.01	39%
Transamerica Premier Equity	71	6.55	34%
Turner Core Growth	83	3.58	104%

None of these Five-Star Large Cap Growth Funds have an R-Squared lower than 53%. Not surprisingly, the average R-Squared of this group is 76%, which means that the overall market does 76% of the portfolio manager's job (on average). The level of annual turnover seems to have very little impact on either performance or R-Squared.

Source: Data from Morningstar, Inc.

TABLE 1.3   R-Squared versus S&P 500, Five-Star **Large Cap Value** Funds, as of February 18, 2006

Fund	3-Yr. R-Squared	3-Yr. Alpha	Annual Turnover
Allianz NJF Dividend Value	82	4.51	30%
Allianz OCC Value	85	1.76	101%
American Beacon Large Cap Value	89	5.27	25%
American Funds Fundamental Inv.	86	3.22	30%
DFA U.S. Large Cap Value	91	3.57	7%
Diamond Hill Large Cap	73	7.90	13%
Dodge & Cox Stock	88	5.05	11%
Dreyfus Premier Strategic Value	88	3.11	123%
Excelsior Value & Restructuring	85	5.65	8%
Fidelity Advisor Cyclical Industrial	79	5.05	116%
Hancock Horizon Value	69	6.27	65%
Hartford Value Opportunities	90	1.94	38%
Hotchkis & Wiley Large Cap Value	76	5.94	14%
John Hancock Classic Value	87	2.70	16%
LSV Value Equity	86	4.66	12%
LWAS/DFA U.S. High Book to Market	91	3.42	7%
Lord Abbett All Value	92	1.20	52%
Merrill Lynch Equity Dividend	65	6.38	4%
Merrill Lynch Large Cap Value	66	7.04	95%
Mutual Shares	83	5.05	33%
Pioneer Cullen Value	81	5.96	49%
RiverSource Diversified Equity Inc.	89	6.30	24%
TCW Galileo Dividend Focused	86	1.40	32%
TIAA-CREF Large Cap Value	90	3.62	113%
Target Large Capitalization Value	87	4.15	47%

The average R-Squared for these Five-Star performers is 83.36%, slightly higher than the Large Cap Growth and Large Cap Blend groups. None of the readings are below 65%. Annual turnover has very little impact on either R-Squared or alpha. In general, value investors seem to have less turnover than growth or blend investors, at least judging by these Five-Star performers.

Source: Data from Morningstar, Inc.

TABLE 1.4   R-Squared versus S&P 500, Five-Star **Small Cap Blend** Funds, as of February 18, 2006

Fund	3-Yr. R-Squared	3-Yr. Alpha	Annual Turnover
American Century Small Cap	71	8.60	123%
Bridgway Ultra Small Company	70	7.16	13%
Constellation Small Cap Value Opp.	67	9.09	193%
Gartmore Small Cap	72	9.88	292%
Hennessy Cornerstone Growth	56	5.60	89%
Keeley Small Cap Value	62	11.33	23%
Lord Abbett Small Cap Blend	66	8.90	59%
Murder Small Cap Value	73	7.40	26%
Neuberger Berman Genesis	62	9.21	11%
Oppenheimer Small & Mid Cap Value	71	10.05	121%
RS Partners	61	15.29	108%
Royce Value	67	14.77	83%
Satuit Capital Micro Cap	59	10.89	184%
Stratton Small Cap Value	65	9.73	17%
T. Rowe Price Small Cap Value	72	7.77	9%
The Boson Company Small Cap Value	73	8.11	51%
Wells Fargo Advantage Small/Mid Cap Value	61	7.84	80%
Wells Fargo Advantage Small Cap Value	62	7.53	33%

In looking at Five-Star Small Cap Blend Funds, I was surprised to see how much more turnover there seems to be than in the Large Cap funds. The turnover doesn't seem to have much added value with this list, which, on average, had an R-Squared of 66.11%. The highest turnover funds, like Gartmore Small Cap and Satuit Capital Micro Cap, did not achieve alphas any better than most of their peers. Only two funds, Hennessy Cornerstone Growth (56%) and Satuit Capital Micro Cap (59%), had R-Squared results less than 60%. Alpha is generally a little higher among these managers versus their large cap counterparts. The last couple of years have, in fact, favored small caps, so these funds' generally higher alphas are not surprising.

Source: Data from Morningstar, Inc.

TABLE 1.5 R-Squared versus S&P 500, Five-Star **Small Cap Growth** Funds, as of February 18, 2006

Fund	3-Yr. R-Squared	3-Yr. Alpha	Annual Turnover
Allianz CCM Emerging Companies	59	4.93	144%
Baron Growth	60	6.65	15%
Baron Small Cap	52	7.07	25%
Bjurman Barry Micro-Cap Growth	61	1.47	28%
Bridgeway Micro Cap Limited	58	8.96	87%
Bridgeway Ultra Small Company	66	8.02	87%
Buffalo Small Cap	69	6.10	35%
Columbia Acorn	79	8.31	20%
Dreyfus Premier Enterprise	65	9.23	157%
FBR Small Cap	65	8.01	19%
Federated Kaufman Small Cap	70	9.34	42%
Gartmore Micro Cap	64	11.38	N/A
JP Morgan Small Cap Equity	69	8.67	44%
Managers AMG Essex Sm/Mic Cp	60	8.30	118%
Munder Micro Cap Equity	65	10.10	36%
Oberweis Micro Cap	56	5.12	58%
Royce Value Plus	65	13.53	56%
Schroder U.S. Opportunities	64	6.99	107%
Turner Micro Cap Growth	68	7.76	74%
Wasatch Micro Cap	62	4.17	50%
Wells Fargo Advantage Sm Cap Opp	64	7.24	7%
Wm Blair Small Cap Growth	68	7.23	109%
Winslow Green Growth	42	11.27	102%

This is the group where one expects to see lower R-Squared statistics, and for this period, at least, that is what we got. A whopping five of these 23 Five-Star funds (just 22%) scored an R-Squared lower than 60. Only one fund, Winslow Green Growth (42%), was lower than 50. Winslow Green Growth's stated investment objective is that it is focused on companies that are "environmentally responsible." Almost 28% of its holdings are concentrated in health-care stocks, the largest sector represented. Not surprisingly, the alpha statistics in this group are among the highest—meaning that they are generally outperforming the overall market. Isn't it interesting that Wells Fargo has virtually no turnover (7%), but has about the same alpha and R-Squared as the average of all the others?
Source: Data from Morningstar, Inc.

TABLE 1.6 R-Squared versus S&P 500, Five-Star **Small Cap Value** Funds, as of February 18, 2006

Fund	3-Yr. R-Squared	3-Yr. Alpha	Annual Turnover
Allianz NFJ Small Cap Value	70	6.39	20%
Diamond Hill Small Cap	64	10.92	24%
Hotchkis & Wiley Small Cap Value	72	10.19	49%
MainStay Small Cap Opportunity	60	10.26	159%
N/I Numeric Investors Sm Cap Value	75	6.44	349%
Pacific Capital Small Cap	77	7.72	68%
Paradigm Value Fund	62	15.69	92%
STI Classic Small Cap Value	73	7.43	17%

None of these Five-Star funds has an R-Squared lower than 60%, which means that the overall market is doing more than 60% of these managers' jobs, too. I marvel that the two lowest alphas (value-added returns) in the group represent opposite ends of the annual turnover extremes!

Source: Data from Morningstar, Inc.

As an aside, I recommend reading Ross Miller's enlightening research paper, "Measuring the True Cost of Active Management by Mutual Funds," published in June 2005 and available at the Social Science Research Network web site, www.ssrn.com. Dr. Miller is an instructor in the Department of Finance at the State University of New York at Albany, and the principal of Miller Risk Advisors (www.miller risk.com).

He notes that while actively managed mutual funds appear to provide investment services in exchange for relatively low fees, *the true cost of active management is understated* because mutual funds bundle passive and active management. He reaches a similar conclusion as I have in writing this book. In reality, he asserts, the average mutual fund will have over 90% of the variance in its returns explained by its benchmark index, which is the passive component.

TABLE 1.7 R-Squared, **Largest** U.S. Stock Funds (Index Funds Excluded), as of February 18, 2006

Fund	3-Yr. R-Squared	3-Yr. Alpha	Annual Turnover
American Funds Growth Fund of America	88	4.24	20%
American Funds Investment Co. of America	93	1.51	19%
Fidelity Contrafund	72	7.69	64%
American Funds Washington Mutual	93	−0.41	16%
Fidelity Magellan	94	−0.28	6%
Dodge & Cox Stock	88	5.05	11%
Fidelity Low-Priced Stock	79	6.00	24%
Fidelity Growth & Income	94	−0.76	31%
Vanguard Windsor	84	3.58	28%
Fidelity Growth Company	73	4.45	50%
Fidelity Equity-Income	95	0.01	19%
American Funds Fundamental Invs.	86	4.17	30%
Fidelity Blue Chip Growth	94	−2.19	29%
Vanguard PRIMECAP	85	4.39	12%
Davis NY Venture	88	3.25	3%
American Century Ultra Inv.	81	−1.89	33%
T. Rowe Price Equity Income	92	0.22	16%
Vanguard Healthcare	47	6.60	13%
Fidelity Dividend Growth	89	−3.36	26%
T. Rowe Price Mid Cap Growth	81	5.86	30%
American Funds Amcap	88	0.56	16%
Fidelity Value	85	6.39	29%
Lord Abbett Affiliated	93	−0.60	49%
American Funds American Mutual	94	0.97	22%
Calamos Growth	61	4.40	63%

The average R-Squared for the 25 largest U.S. funds is 85%, which means that the market's concurrent performance explains roughly 85% of the performance of these large funds. With the exception of Vanguard Healthcare (47%), Calamos Growth (61%), Fidelity Contrafund (72%), Fidelity Growth Company (73%), and Fidelity Low-Priced Stock (79%), these large funds have performances that are more than 80% explained by the S&P 500, according to Morningstar's R-Squared statistic. Here, the funds with marginally higher annual turnover rates seem to have slightly higher alphas.

Source: Data from Morningstar, Inc.

His paper describes a method for *decomposing* the elements of fund management, and for allocating fund expenses between active and passive management. Then he constructs a simple formula for finding a more accurate cost of the active management portion of performance to answer the questions: How much difference is the active manager really making, and how much is it really costing the investor?

Dr. Miller's "active expense ratio," when applied to the universe of mutual funds, is enlightening. For example, at the end of 2004, the mean active expense ratio (his calculation) for the large cap equity mutual funds tracked by Morningstar was about 7.00%—*over six times their published mean expense ratio of 1.15%.* "More broadly," he concludes, "funds in the Morningstar universe had a mean active expense ratio of 5.2%, while the largest funds averaged a percent or two less. . . . Although the manager may *intend* (emphasis added) to provide his investors with 100% active management, his intentions are not the issue when his actions can be replicated at a significantly lower cost via indexing."

Okay, so the first problem traditional investors face if their ambition truly is to earn superior investment returns is that most often they are *only* buying good companies. As we have seen, that's not enough because how the investment portfolios are comprised is not nearly as important as overall stock market direction. Not by a long shot.

This brings us to the *second problem* among traditional managers today when it comes to achieving superior investment results: *The financial services industry has oversold the concept of diversification.* As a result, most managers' long-only portfolios or mutual funds might as well be the S&P 500 or another benchmark index, simply because today's portfolios are too broadly diversified to gain a meaningful performance advantage over the competition.

Too much of what America (and the world) has been sold as active management is really *closet indexing*. Labeling the effort as active management may allow the advisory firm to charge a higher fee, but labels don't help the fund's performance rise above mediocrity.

FIVE-STAR CONCENTRATION

What really sets apart the five-star managers with lower R-Squared ratings is that they are not afraid of concentrating a good chunk of assets into relatively few stocks or a very few industry sectors. If you need a model for this concept, let's start with the Vanguard Healthcare fund. It's one of the 25 largest U.S. funds, according to Morningstar, and it carries a five-star rating for its historical performance—but of course 91% of its holdings are concentrated in the Health sector.

The good news for the fund's investors is that in the past few years, the Healthcare sector has done quite well. We all seem quite willing to spend a lot of money on extending our lives and looking good while doing so! If the sector ever falls out of favor among investors, then this fund will probably suffer in terms of its performance because it is a specialty sector fund and, by charter, not able to stray very far from its healthcare focus. Consequently, its "stars" stand to lose some of their luster when the industry becomes overpriced—or we collectively decide that there is no merit in trying to live longer, or somebody at last finds Juan Ponce de Leon's long-sought Fountain of Youth in the swamps of Florida!

A sector-focused fund cannot diversify very much outside their chosen industry category, but what about those five-star performers without such limitations, those who chose to go out on a limb to stand head and shoulders above their competitors?

One of the five-star performers among the 25 largest U.S. funds is the Fidelity Contrafund, whose lead manager is William Danhoff. While Morningstar lists the Contrafund among its Large Cap Growth funds, the descriptions available at both Morningstar and Fidelity Investments' web sites emphasize the unrecognized "fundamental value" aspects of the companies in which the Danhoff-led team invests.

What really separates Contrafund from its peers, though, is an R-Squared of only 70%, which is quite low for such a large fund ($63.8 billion in assets as of February 28, 2006). How did megafund "Contra" post such a low (relative) R-Squared and achieve alpha of +7.69, a performance far better than the other 24 largest funds? It had *large, above-average sector concentrations* in Energy, Healthcare, Information Technology, and Financials, according to the publicly available Morningstar data. So it was really not that well diversified, after all. And that deemphasis of diversification is one of the potential tickets to earning superior investment results.

In the tables above, I did not include the Five-Star funds in Morningstar's Mid-Cap Blend, Mid-Cap Growth and Mid-Cap Value categories, but the R-Squared rankings generally fell between the Large Cap and Small Cap funds, which represent the opposite ends of the traditional money management spectrum.

I would be remiss if I didn't spotlight Ken Heebner's CGM Focus fund, which falls into the Mid-Cap Blend category and is five-star rated. And at just 35%, the R-Squared of CGM Focus was among the lowest in the entire mutual fund universe, *and its alpha was a whopping 13.12*. How did Mr. Heebner achieve superior performance that is *not* mostly dependent on the overall market?

Well, consider that as of February 28, 2006, a full 77% of CGM Focus holdings were concentrated in a single sector, Manufacturing, which included a little more than 33% of fund assets in Industrial Materials and almost 40% concentrated in Energy stocks. Once again, there was a performance gain by deemphasizing diversification.

Keep in mind that these very few funds have *ignored* the financial services industry's mantra in the past 20 years that *broad diversification* is the preferred way of stock market investing. Few brave souls, like Mr. Danhoff and Mr. Heebner, have been unafraid to make big bets in one or a few industry groups, or a smaller number of stocks, putting money and commitment behind the strength of their convictions. If they are right about the industry group(s) or individual stocks with their concentrations, their mutual funds become five-star performers. If they are wrong, then maybe they become one-star performers, but at least they are putting their money where their advertised skill set is. They are at least *trying* to earn their premium management fees.

Why does a mutual fund investor pay the "active manager premium" if not to distinguish his investment performance from all the others, hopefully head and shoulders above the competition? Because for the last two or three decades the investment industry has told investors, "broad diversification is the way to go." If the mutual fund investor aspires toward mediocrity, he has achieved his objective.

As Yale University's Mr. Swenson said, "Many try, but few succeed in winning the active management game." It is no small wonder that indexing has grown in popularity when, in most years, the vast majority of traditional active managers fail to outperform the market averages. The indexing investor at least *knows* that he is going to get mediocre investment results. And sadly, he *smiles* at having achieved mediocrity.

Throw away the shackles of your investing past, and read on! This book is about achieving superior investment performance. By absorbing the most important factors that influence performance, you are well on your way toward enhanced returns and better management of investment risk—whether you are a portfolio manager or an individual investor.

2

This Is Not Your Grandfather's Stock Market

If you pin them down, most professional money managers admit that the overall stock market's performance is the major driver of almost any well-diversified portfolio's performance: It's hard to contradict all of the academic studies and performance analytics that support this claim.

In fact, what most professional managers are really doing is chasing "alpha," the statistical tool we discussed in Chapter 1 that is used by analytical firms to evaluate how much risk-adjusted, value-added the manager is actually providing over and above the market. *Investopedia.com* explains that "a positive alpha is the extra return awarded to the investor for taking additional risk rather than accepting the market return."

The major reason so many traditional active managers underperform the overall market and earn negative alphas is because they are stuck in a time warp; they were taught to only "buy good companies." A good company will see its share price increase in value over the long-term. Maybe the intrinsic value or net worth of the company is increasing because of the reinvestment of profits. Or maybe the company is paying out a large portion of its profits in dividends and investors will "pay up" for that potentially increasing return of cash flow. Conventional wisdom suggests that eventually these good companies' corporate performance or generosity to their shareholders will be reflected in higher share prices.

Buyers of good companies have been coached to hold these positions through every kind of market environment—up, down, and sideways. And since the regulatory environment in which traditional managers operate encourages a long-only investment approach (no short selling and few hedging choices), *their only way to earn positive alpha is to be a better stock picker.*

Because of size issues, the traditional manager of long-only mutual funds who has a better chance of making a difference in all market environments is the manager who concentrates the fund's assets in a very few industry groups. They are the groups that his research says are growing in favor and likely to see an extended period of price appreciation. While diversification helps manage risk, *too much diversification is counterproductive.* It leads to mediocre or sub-par performance. Diversification to the extent it is being practiced today doesn't really give investors the added value they are supposedly paying for.

LOGIC MANDATES OTHER SOLUTIONS

We will discuss in greater detail elsewhere in this book that there are only three basic ways to achieve superior results and move away from the mediocre performance sold so effectively by the investment industry.

It's really pretty simple. If too much diversification leads to mediocrity, then the first two ways toward superior returns are to reduce the level of diversification.

First, you can concentrate your assets in just a scant few companies and really do your homework on those targeted for investment. This is not practical for most professional money managers because they simply have too much capital to put to work. And it isn't practical for any but a few individual investors because most don't have the skills or the time to analyze the quality of the enterprise, as well as its *relative* current valuation vs. its potential valuation.

The second way to superior returns is more practical, and in fact is already being pursued by money managers like Fidelity's Danhoff and CGM's Heebner in the management of Five-Star funds. These managers are focusing their attention and capital commitments to broad sector themes, like energy, commodities, or healthcare. They achieve a degree of diversification by investing in several companies within a sector, and even more risk is spread by committing capital to, say, three or four primary sectors being emphasized, not just one.

But isn't it also logical that *if the overall market is the major driver* of performance in a well-diversified portfolio that a *third solution* aimed at superior performance might be even more effective? That you should (1) develop methodologies for establishing the probability of overall market direction; and then (2) use some sort of hedging, trading, or investment strategies to take advantage? But no, the traditional active managers' forefathers managed long-only portfolios of good companies through markets thick and thin, so long-only active management is the best way to earn generous investment returns. See, Grandpa is smiling!

Well, tough; this is not your grandfather's market. *Financial news and information is more rapidly and more widely disseminated* than our grandfathers ever imagined in their wildest dreams. Can you imagine what Thomas Jefferson or Ben Franklin would do with a BlackBerry? Decision makers around the world have, at their fingertips, detailed access to event information and analysis *as it is unfolding*, and can communicate their impressions before the event has grown cold.

I will never forget turning on the television to learn that a jetliner had crashed into one of the World Trade Center towers just moments before. And then, right before my horrified eyes, the world witnessed live, up close, personal, and in color, a second airliner as it approached, then crashed into the other WTC tower in a ball of flames.

As events unfold, experts are immediately on the radio and television airwaves interpreting the impact and consequences of the crisis, the achievement, or the mere moment. Efficient market theorists should be proud. Sometimes offsetting analysis and contradictory opinions are simultaneously so pervasive that markets are paralyzed by investors' collective uncertainty.

And Grandpa takes another swig of Appalachian moonshine. *Regulatory initiatives* implemented in 1975 switched the brokerage industry from *fixed* to *negotiated* commissions. This simple act launched a never-before-seen wave of price competition in brokerage firms' commissions. In fact, it led to the "commoditization" of security trade execution. Discount firms popped up, like Charles Schwab, Jack White, Olde Discount, and La Salle Street Securities. Then online brokerages, like Scottrade, e-Trade, and Ameritrade pressed the revenue models of the financial services industry even further downward.

As a consequence, the profit in brokerage commissions for trade execution all but evaporated. So with declining profit margin in commissions, beginning in the 1980s "full-service" brokerage firms developed new, asset-based fee structures around new, *asset-gathering* sales models.

Our grandfathers often made investment decisions after reading full-service firms' research reports. Well, with diminishing profit margins in trade execution, even large investment houses like Goldman Sachs, Merrill Lynch, and UBS severely curtailed or eliminated equity research as a client service. In today's larger, more highly liquid markets (in part born of the lower trading costs), the big investment houses make more money through their trading desks *not* by charging the less-than-one-cent-per-share commissions that price competition mandates, but by "proprietary trading," which often amounts to nothing more than taking in blocks of stock at the "bid" and flipping them out minutes later at the "ask" for maybe five (or more) cents higher (or five times the commission they *might* have earned on the same trade)!

And *the tax environment is much less onerous* than our grandfathers knew. *Trading* creates short-term gains or losses. Net short-term gains are taxed as ordinary income. For taxable accounts, the highest income tax bracket today is an effective rate of 39.6% following President Clinton's 1993 initiative to raise rates, but this is still substantially less onerous to short-term trading profits than the 50, 70, and even 90% levels our grandfathers experienced, according to a history of taxation found at the U.S. Department of the Treasury's web site. Yes, it's true: A progressive income tax with a high-end tax rate of 90% was a reality of our grandfathers' lifetimes. Certainly it made them think long and hard about abandoning one investment, however overvalued it might have been, for another.

There are legislative initiatives promoted today that, if enacted, would eliminate the 15% long-term capital gains tax completely. This would further lessen the financial challenges for anyone wanting to sell one stock investment in favor of another, or to reallocate capital to other asset classes or other uses.

And, of course, Grandpa didn't have an Individual Retirement Account (IRA), 401(k), or other tax-qualified retirement plan. With these, *the tax trigger is neither the act of liquidating nor how long you hold a stock.* Most qualified plans have rendered irrelevant the question of tax consequences for liquidating a stock investment. Today, people can reposition the investments inside of their tax-qualified "umbrella" and not worry about the tax consequences until they withdraw money from the account.

Exchange-traded derivatives didn't exist way back in Granddad's day. *Now there are equity and index options on hundreds of individual stocks and indexes* at the Chicago Board Options Exchange, the American Stock Exchange, the Philadelphia Exchange, the International Securities Exchange, and the Pacific Stock Exchange. *Billions of dollars in index futures* (and options on futures) change hands every day at the Chicago Mercantile Exchange, the Chicago Board of Trade, the Eurex U.S., and the New York Board of Trade, not to mention at exchanges in London, Hong Kong, Sydney, Tokyo, and a host of other countries.

Then there are the relative new kids on the block, *exchange-traded funds (ETFs)*, which have gained widespread market acceptance and *are now traded on almost every major index and industry group*, in almost every major international marketplace. Both leveraged and unleveraged mutual fund indexing models, trading billions upon billions of dollars, have been built around the ETFs' short existence. To be sure, derivatives like ETFs and index futures facilitate hedging, they facilitate speculation— and they have contributed to increased market liquidity compared to what Grandpa knew.

The 2005 merger of the New York Stock Exchange with Archipelago Holdings, Inc. transitions the granddaddy of stock exchanges from non-profit to for-profit status—and launches the Big Board's trading front and center into the electronic age. Since the Buttonwood Agreement in 1792 created the Exchange, the NYSE's trading has required some degree of face-to-face interaction between buyer and seller, or representatives thereof, at a physical location. First that physical location was under the fabled Buttonwood Tree; then trading migrated to the Exchange floor.

Technology improvements, especially in the past 20 years, have rendered obsolete the inflection in one's voice or a raised eyebrow. For today's electronic trading networks like Arca/Ex, Island, Bloomberg Tradebook, REDIBook, Instinet, and Strike, or electronic exchanges like NASDAQ, there are simply too many humans on a physical exchange floor. Humans get in the way of good, best-price execution. Moreover, having to manually write trade tickets with the human hand is an inhibitor to trading volume, which has to be ever faster and ever greater for anybody to make money of any consequence in execution, given the low transaction fees now attached!

Low transaction costs and a lower tax environment, *combined with new computer-based technologies that facilitate instantaneous execution online*, also opens up a whole new industry of proprietary and high-frequency trading. With firms like Scottrade offering $7 commissions for any size or-der, America's Everyman can clip the market's intraday volatility for much more than a fair day's wage on relatively small amounts of capital. By trading just 1,000 shares, the Scottrade commission amounts to about a penny and a half per share as the cost of doing business *for the buy and the sell combined.*

Grandpa would have loved it. From a business modeling perspective, let's say you make just five cents per share profit (gross revenues) on the trade, minus the penny and a half commission (your cost of sales). This means your gross operating margin on your trading business is 70%. Many enterprises around the world would be envious of a 70% gross margin! Now you just have to *consistently* trade profitably so that your cumulative gross margin covers your "SG&A" (selling, general, and administrative ex-penses on a corporate income statement).

The trade execution for online trading is often instantaneous and no more than three or four seconds for market orders. And online, real-time graphics packages based on a wide array of both technical and fundamen-tal analysis give the little guy, with the nimbleness from being small, a deci-sive edge over many of the institutions in today's more liquid marketplace.

No, this is not your grandfather's stock market. Regulatory reforms de-mand full and fair disclosure of public company information and greater fiduciary responsibilities to be exercised by corporate executives privy to in-side information. Some in the public markets have suggested that Sarbanes-Oxley went too far and has proven too expensive for many public companies, but certainly it has raised the bar of fair play.

All investors are now entitled to accurate facts, figures, and guidance, not just research analysts and large institutional investors. The cigar-smoke-filled backrooms our grandfathers knew have been replaced by openly aired, quarterly conference calls after an earnings report. Does it still happen that an analyst or institutional investor gets privileged infor-mation? Absolutely! But it is not supposed to be, and those so engaged (both giving and receiving privileged information) suffer harsh penalties if caught. Material information is supposed to be transparent to *all* investors.

At risk of oversimplification, I offer that the history of professional stock market investing has evolved in three distinct waves.

First Wave investors had virtually no choice but to adopt *long-term, buy-and-hold investment strategies because high commission costs and the taxable consequences of selling discouraged shorter-term trading.* First Wave professional managers were motivated no differently. They had to deal with the same obstacles of commissions and taxes on behalf of their clients.

Consequently, active managers simply aspired to construct portfolios of the best companies they could find with above-average prospects. During this developmental phase, with the broadening acceptance of professional portfolio management and intensifying competition, managers began to differentiate themselves through strategies, styles, and stock selection methods.

But as funds and managed accounts got bigger and active managers made investment decisions for larger pools of capital, it became harder and harder to find enough investment opportunities. In the late 1990s, I was talking with a high-profile portfolio manager in Boston about the dearth of "good ideas" (companies) available either for research or investment. He said, "You know, when I first got into the management business in the early 1980s, my biggest problem was having a lot of great ideas but not enough capital to invest. Today, our biggest challenge is the reverse. We have enormous amounts of capital assets to put to work, but not enough good ideas."

In other words, there are not enough "good companies" to own. So how does a manager deploy surplus capital that he is charged by clients to invest in equities? Of course, he has to invest in an increased number of companies, many of which he may judge to be only mediocre opportunities. So he is sorely tempted to blunt the added risk by even more broadly diversifying his holdings. The result is blunted performance.

By the 1980s, pension investors became frustrated with most active managers' failure to match the market averages, much less beat them. Almost every year, there are estimates suggesting that *more than 80% of traditional active managers fail to at least match the market averages' performance*. Should it be surprising, then, that pension fund trustees question paying active managers premium management fees for *under*-performance?

So the Second Wave was born when *advanced mathematical models and computer technology facilitated the concept of indexing*. Especially with the introduction of index futures and index options, indexing gained meaningful traction in the early to mid-1980s. With indexing, investors didn't have to worry about beating the market averages. With indexing, they aspire only to mediocrity and, by and large, they get better performance than the 80% of traditional active managers who annually underperform the indexes.

The indexing manager is not paid to analyze business models and company prospects, or to choose between alternatives. He does not advertise himself as "a better stock picker." He simply buys the companies in the assigned index. Consequently, the fees he charges his investment clients are lower, too.

And yet, the market seems to have grown increasingly volatile in the past 30 years. Periods of bear market adversity, such as 1987, the early 1990s, and 2000 to 2003, certainly brought *increased attention to market risk*.

Indexing may solve the related problems of underperformance and high fees, but it does absolutely nothing to address the very real problems of volatility and risk—nor does it hold out the promise of above-average, much less superior investment returns. Investors today clamor for more effective management of market risk *and* they want better-than-market returns. Can they have their cake and eat it, too?

MIRROR, MIRROR ON THE WALL . . .

I believe they can, but it takes a different approach than has traditionally been offered by the financial services industry. With few exceptions, traditional active managers do very little to manage risk other than, ostensibly, to "own the best companies" and to construct a well-diversified portfolio. On the surface, those are laudable objectives. But as my orthopedic surgeon discovered, buying and holding even diversified portfolios of the presumed best companies will see valuations get *crushed* during periods of market adversity.

Now we are well into the Third Wave of stock market investing. Investors do, indeed, want to have their cake and eat it, too. Yes, they want superior, above-market returns and they want more effective risk management—neither of which they are likely to experience with traditional portfolio management methods. They don't have to accept at face value their financial planner's counsel to manage stock market risk by having a bunch of their *other* money in real estate or some other asset class. You can manage risk more effectively than your grandfather ever dreamed possible by thinking conceptually and strategically, and using a little common sense.

Historians will look back and say that the first decade of the twenty-first century was when investors big and small turned to "alternative investing" with strident enthusiasm. In the early part of this decade, well-heeled, "accredited" investors and pension funds were throwing money at proprietary investment and trading partnerships, colloquially known as "hedge funds." According to an article by John Rubino in the August 2005 issue of *CFA* magazine, "The Once and Future King," from 2000 to 2005 the number of hedge funds worldwide rose from 5,000 to 8,000, while managed assets doubled, to over $1 trillion. According to Rubino, "Hedge funds now account for more than half the daily volume on the New York Stock Exchange. . . . And close to one-fourth of Wall Street's profit comes from lending to, trading for, and advising hedge funds."

Put in perspective, hedge funds have collectively become a significant economic force with which to reckon. And yet, a mere trillion dollars in assets is still tiny when compared to the overall amounts invested in stocks and bonds, including in the traditional, underperforming mutual funds of our grandfathers. So the hedge funds of today have only scratched the surface of their impact potential. There is plenty of room left for accelerating growth. And, if I am right, in the not terribly distant future there will be few distinguishable differences between hedge funds and the trappings taken on by many traditional mutual funds as they evolve in response to the competition.

Hedge funds became the darlings of Wall Street for good reason. Freed of mutual fund charters and excessive regulation about the strategies they might implement, hedge funds provide accredited investors with leveraged or defensive portfolio opportunities that can profit throughout the various market cycles—up, down, and sideways. And every hedge fund manager strives to achieve the objectives of better performance with less risk in a different way, with a different strategy, and even with different investment vehicles.

Whether or not they have the right strategy, hedge fund managers have a much better probability of achieving investment nirvana—*better performance and better risk management*—than do their traditional manager counterparts. Why? Simply because they don't have to be long-only, fully invested in stocks.

Some equity-oriented hedge funds engage only in "paired trades" or "market-neutral" strategies. Others specialize in investing in the securities of distressed companies. Many engage in high-frequency or day-trading strategies using large cap stocks. Still others make concentrated, leveraged bets in specific market sectors or industries. And an increasing number have started taking an activist approach, seeking to influence a company's management once they purchase a sizable equity stake. To be quite honest, the term *hedge funds* is a misnomer in today's world, because they are about earning superior, value-added returns and not just about blunting risk.

And importantly, only hedge funds and enlightened individual investors, not the traditionalists, are able to *use the overall market direction instead of being its victim* with some of the concepts, strategies, and tactics discussed in this book. That is, until the traditional management companies change their investment charters.

This thought arose recently in my conversation with a very successful Boston-based, traditional long-only manager. He offered that fewer than 5% of the long-only managers operating today use any kind of risk management mechanism other than "owning the best companies." Their mandate is to be 100% long stocks. Some will raise cash positions when they fear market adversity, but holding 10% or more cash at any time is considered by many academicians and asset allocation specialists to be "style drift," and reason for criticism. A few, he said, will write covered calls, the practice of selling to someone else the right to buy your stock at a specified exercise price within a certain period of time. In exchange, the option seller receives an agreed-upon amount of money (most often facilitated by market prices on a listed options exchange), called a premium. For more information on covered option writing, go online to www.optionsclearing.com and request a copy of their brochures, Understanding Stock Options and Understanding Index Options, and the booklet, *Characteristics and Risks of Standardized Options*.

Still fewer advisors engage in buying put options ("portfolio insurance") in their managed funds or accounts but, the Boston manager said, "You are seeing an increasing number use alternative means, whether buying puts or selling covered calls, because they have to do more than just be long-only. Just like they were once forced to advertise themselves as better stock pickers because of an investment style or research method, today they have to somehow differentiate themselves from the crowd—with better performance and reduced asset volatility—to compete for assets."

In fact, the traditional, long-only management industry as we've known it is an aged, if not dying profession. We are already seeing symptoms. The costs of managing a fund or traditional advisory operation are rising even as compensation is getting squeezed. *Management services have become commoditized, largely by the push toward diversification and indexing*. Investors are increasingly voting with their pocketbooks, unwilling to pay premium management fees to active managers unable to add value greater than what the market, in general, is offering.

To achieve economies of scale, funds are being merged as asset management companies consolidate. Blackrock, Inc.'s announced merger with Merrill Lynch Investment Managers in February 2006—to form a $1 trillion investment management firm—is just one highly visible event in this wave of consolidation. Later in the same month, publicly traded Boston Private Financial Holdings, Inc. (NASDAQ: BPFH), announced its intention to acquire majority ownership of Boston-based Anchor Capital and sister management firm Anchor/Russell. Combined, the Anchor management firms being acquired had roughly $4.55 billion under management on the day of the news announcement. As in every other industry, this consolidation allows the merged firms to benefit from the efficiencies resulting from economies of scale, with hopes that their merged corporate cultures can coexist.

MABEL, THE BARN'S ON FIRE

While traditional management companies band together to make ends meet, large investors (individual and institutional) increasingly seek low-fee indexing alternatives. Beyond indexing, more and more they are turning to hedge funds, because indexing does not address the problem of market volatility. Hedge funds can.

But securities laws prevent all but accredited investors (institutions or very-high-net-worth individuals) from investing in hedge funds. So for the "commoner," new varieties of mutual funds and mutual fund asset allocation strategies have gained market traction in this third wave of stock market investing. Ironically, as you will see in Act II, traditional active managers with a pledge to be long-only equities can also find a potential, if backhanded solution for competing more effectively among the new varieties of investment management alternatives.

Today, mutual fund companies like Rydex Investments, ProFunds, and the relative newcomer, Direxionfunds, make available just about every conceivable kind of equity index fund. Own *Rydex OTC*, and you own an unleveraged portfolio of growth stocks comprising the NASDAQ 100. Buy *Rydex Nova*, and you own a modestly leveraged portfolio based on the Standard & Poor's 500. Purchase *Rydex Ursa*, and you will profit on a decline in the S&P 500, but you will lose money if the overall market rises.

You are not an accredited investor and so are unable to buy into a hedge fund directly? Well, Rydex even allows you to invest in mutual funds that are tied to the performance of several hedge funds, *indirectly* opening up this important Third Wave investment vehicle to the uncommon commoner.

And then there are the sector funds. You think gold is going to $1,000 per ounce? Mrs. John Q. Public can buy the *Rydex Precious Metals Fund*. There is an energy shortage, you say? Well then invest in *Rydex Energy* or *Rydex Energy Services*, because they should do well in a period of rising oil and gas prices. You can find similar industry-specific funds at the likes of Vanguard, Fidelity, ProFunds, AIM, Blackrock, Dreyfus, Allianz, Franklin, Gartmore, ING, Ivy, and many other mutual fund families. By focusing on sectors and doing your research, you might even be able to achieve the same kind of less-diversified, above-average performance as Fidelity's Danhoff and CGM's Heebner.

Still clinging to your financial planner's advice and not sure you want to put all your eggs in one basket? Well then, asset allocation models make modified, hedge fund–type investing strategies accessible to mainstream America, not just to the accredited affluent. The allocation strategies offered by professional investment advisors vary. Some use tactical strategies based on market movement and the performance of asset classes within defined time periods. Others depend on the not-so-simple art of market timing.

In addition to earning potentially more generous returns, a frequently cited objective of timing-derived mutual fund allocation strategies is to take the "canyons" and "valleys" out of the mutual fund portfolio's performance picture. In other words, you can more effectively manage market risk, and you may even enhance your return potential in the process!

WIDE OPEN, GUNS BLAZING

The early pioneers heralded by Frederic Jackson Turner's "frontier thesis" of American history must have wondered whether the risks they were taking in settling the wilds of the West would be worth it in the long-term. Of course, they had no idea that their venturesome homesteading would lead to the discovery of abundant natural resources with which to build this great country and help forge a national culture based on capitalism and market-driven investment dynamics.

Alternative investing is the financial services industry's new frontier, represented by hedge funds and mutual fund-based, *active* asset allocation models.

Critics abound. They suggest that the whole hedge fund fervor will eventually blow up in our collective faces because of excessive leverage in the marketplace. They advance that hedge funds pose a threat to the entire economic and financial system. Many also point out that the concentrated sector investments of managers like CGM's Mr. Heebner and Fidelity Investments' Mr. Danhoff put investors at much greater risk.

Maybe, but it is exercising that kind of value-added judgment for which they are receiving premium compensation. The multitude of closet indexers, on the other hand, with R-Squared statistics approaching or exceeding 90%, deserve compensation more closely resembling real indexers.

Sure, I am concerned that some new hedge fund managers are occasionally getting funded with millions of dollars in "seed" or "incubator" capital, even though they may be fresh out of school with hardly a clue as to what makes a market go up and down. I bless them for their opportunity, but wonder about their long-term prospects.

Sure, there are a lot of hedge fund failures, just like in every other business, whether a startup auto repair shop or a Starbucks wannabe. Over the past three years, an estimated 30% of new hedge funds failed, according to the aforementioned articles in CFA magazine.

Some fail because of bad performance. Others fail because they can't raise enough capital, or they don't have the staying power to reach critical mass. Still others fall by the wayside because the market inefficiency of their strategy becomes efficient—and they don't figure out any other inefficiencies of which to take advantage.

But most hedge fund managers are very smart guys. Many are succeeding because these seasoned professionals have a vision for earning above-average, steady returns. Managing risk is equally important to them. By charter, they often have the ability to use leverage if appropriate, but the vast majority of modern hedge fund managers are *not* the "gunslingers" and "wildcatters" that marked the early days of hedge fund management. We are unlikely to see the likes of another George Soros or Julian Robertson come along, guys who made large, superleveraged bets on single investment themes—guys who won and lost small fortunes in silver, or antagonized whole nation-states by betting against their currencies.

In general, those aren't the managers that are getting funded today, not by the serious money, anyway. However successful some of the hedge fund

pioneers were, today's professionals are finding an important balance between return objectives, how much risk and asset volatility are acceptable,
and their fiduciary responsibilities while earning premium, incentive-laden
compensation. And of course, a lot this is driven by the institutional investors and pension funds providing the investment and trading capital.

During my Chicago years (in the 1980s and early 1990s), I met a
young mathematician from the University of Illinois who parlayed new
theories of options and futures risk into helping build a highly profitable,
proprietary trading firm. Some folks out of business school sell technology,
financial services, or industrial equipment. My friend simply sells volatility
and risk, and earns a generous return in doing so.

In North Carolina, I met a successful textile company executive who
saw the proverbial "writing on the wall" in that industry's growing international competition. So he cashed out at an opportune time and adapted
his interest in the stock market to a second career as a hedge fund manager.
He is methodically learning his new trade and rethinking his early percep-
tions about the investing process. In addition to learning about new investment strategies, he is becoming a better trader/investor by attending
seminars on market psychology and workshops on better managing risk—
and his fund's dramatically improved financial performance is testimony to
his will and commitment to a continuing education.

In New York, I know a former Wall Street brokerage firm's head trader
who left his job executing customer orders to launch a successful hedge
fund specializing in high-frequency trading models. And in another financial center, the director of a major university's Master of Science degree
program in investment management left academia to bring his learned discipline to the process of *evaluating* hedge funds for prospective funding by
a multibillion-dollar "fund of hedge funds."

The hedge fund industry is growing up. Not only will it continue to
grow, it will flourish. There is so much diversity in hedge fund strategies
that economic or financial failure of one fund is *not* likely to be problematic for the rest of the industry, much less the broader economy.

Just as with the traditional, long-only managers, some hedge fund
companies are pursuing similar strategies with similar trading vehicles.
There are differences between the traditional funds in style and research
method, but many of them have stock portfolios that are similarly constructed. A hiccup at General Motors or Delta Airlines affects many, simultaneously. And, of course, if the overall stock market goes into a
tailspin, nearly all traditional, long-only managers tend to suffer. In fact,

many traditional managers even aggravate any downward market spiral with panic selling.

One of my institutional research clients in Boston concurred with me about the diminishing valued-added brought to the marketplace by traditional, long-only investment managers, largely because of the overemphasis on diversification that has made them all so much the same. He recently commented, "Look, if the large pension fund investors get fed up, if they become aware of what they are really getting, or really *not* getting, and decide to leave those traditional managers in droves, what's going to happen? They are fully invested. If clients want to pull out, the portfolio managers have to liquidate stocks. Where are those large blocks of stock going to go? At what price?

"If and when that kind of exodus occurs," he said, "there is going to be a huge displacement of equities in the financial markets and a long period of valuation uncertainty."

To this point, I offer that *many equity-oriented hedge fund strategies and nearly all traditional portfolio managers could benefit from an increased awareness and sensitivity to overall stock market direction before it becomes problematic.* It is the most important driver of any well-diversified stock portfolio's performance—whether the portfolio is predominantly long or short individual stocks. It only makes sense to get this important performance factor working *for* you, rather than against you.

As I write this book, the inflows of capital to the hedge fund industry have slowed down a bit because 2005 was a challenging year for traditional and hedge fund managers alike in earning above-market-average returns. Well-heeled people (and the pension institutions they run) don't pay high fees for mediocrity, at least not for very long. Unless you are generating extremely high returns, fairly consistently, the standard "1 to 2% annual management fee versus 20% of profits" hedge fund compensation model may be viewed as unwarranted compensation in light of who is taking the risk.

As the hedge fund industry matures and many of the market inefficiencies that they identify and take advantage of disappear, I look for hedge fund executives to realize they are human, too. They will seek still rich, but lower pay structures. I have already heard instances of incentive fees being lowered from what used to be a standard 20%, to as low as 10% of new profits. Soon they will be offering their services for 5% of new profits—and, I'll bet, control increasingly larger pools of pension and institutional capital. In industry after industry, competitive forces tend to drive compensation models downward and toward a more universal market acceptance. The hedge fund industry is no different. What is fair? The marketplace will decide.

But rest assured: This is not your grandfather's stock market. Alternative investing has taken hold. Hedge funds and mutual fund asset allocation strategies are simple and obvious forms of alternative investing. I venture to say that the performance gaps between alternative and traditional approaches will continue to push traditional active managers in the alternative direction.

There are other, more esoteric forms of alternative investing, and they have witnessed increasing market acceptance in recent years, too. They include opportunities in private equity financing, venture capital, leveraged buyouts, active trading of exchange-traded funds, currency overlays, commodity pools, precious metals, real estate, antiques, and fine art. Auto racing enthusiasts even buy and sell NASCAR collectibles on e-Bay!

For purposes of this book, right now alternative managers are the only way that investors seeking professional help can find advisors who operate on knowledge of a simple truth that the single most important factor in the performance of *any* well-diversified portfolio is the direction of the overall stock market. We'll address solutions in later chapters, but first we have one more dragon to slay.

3

The Farce That Is
"Buy and Hold"

Even today, many investment industry professionals tout the virtues of the buy-good-companies-and-hold-them-for-the-long-term philosophy. Over time, they say, a well-diversified portfolio of stocks will outperform most other asset classes.

I have attended scores of presentations by mutual fund wholesalers, where the virtues of long-only, well-diversified equity portfolios have been extolled based on the long-term performance of the Standard & Poor's 500 Stock Index. Very often, these wholesalers trot out charts compiled by Ibbotson & Associates, a Chicago-based firm with analytical studies of various asset classes and that sells related software and other products.

Ironically, a great deal of Ibbotson's very fine academic work that is published on the firm's web site (www.ibbotson.com) is *not* to extol the virtues of a buy-and-hold philosophy. Rather, *it is to convince readers of the value added in pursuing strategic asset allocation models with their investments in a diverse mix of asset classes.*

Much to their credit, Ibbotson makes the case that financial goals can be achieved with better risk management by balancing, and even periodically rebalancing, investments across three basic asset classes: stocks, bonds, and money market. More recently, they stress that adding additional asset classes, such as precious metals, real estate, and a basket of commodities, does an even better job of risk management without sacrificing much in the way of returns, if any.

I will touch on asset allocation models in later chapters, but first I want to lay bare the realities of a buy-and-hold investment approach. It just doesn't wash as a practical investment strategy *unless you are pursuing only lackluster results*—not in this age of fast-changing business models, accelerated product obsolescence, increased market volatility, low commissions, and so many varieties of tax-deferred accounts. Moreover, the performance data that is used to support the basic buy-and-hold premise is quite flawed. The more cynical might assert that not only is the performance data commonly used to support buy and hold flawed, but *it borders on fraudulent* because it is often not about buying and holding at all!

Investing in good companies is a laudable objective. In fact, buying good companies should be the cornerstone of portfolio construction. If you invest in a good company, the thinking goes, then "Father Time" will eventually bail you out if the share price initially declines. So, buy and hold, right?

Wrong. I'll touch on portfolio construction, market timing, and repositioning in subsequent chapters. Right now, let's look at the flawed reasoning and dubious evidence used to support buy and hold.

Let's grant for a moment that you invested in one of the stock market averages. George Muzea ("The Magic T") refers somewhat cynically to most investors as part of "the trivial many." They are invariably late to the party. They don't get enthusiastic about stocks until near the end of a secular bull market (i.e., 1973, 1999). These investors may not break even on their buy-and-hold positions for well over 10 years, maybe longer.

The jury is still out, of course, on the poor suckers who bought stocks in late 1999 or early 2000, on when they might break even. It might be 10 years, it might be 5 years. It might be 20 years. Maybe one day their stocks will recover the value of their investment(s), maybe not. In some instances, they might never break even because their "good companies" are bankrupt (a number of dot-bombs and technology stocks come to mind, and a highly touted energy behemoth that sounds like "Enron").

Has anybody tried to sell *buy and hold* to shareholders of Ford and General Motors lately? For buyers of U.S. Steel in May 1993, it would be almost 12 years before they broke even at the end of 2004, but by July 2005 they were already back to "under water"! Now, in early 2006, what Grandpa simply called "Steel" is again challenging (but has not exceeded) its early 2005 highs, but so many of the 1993 investors are *still* behind.

Okay, so there are risks in using buy and hold for an individual stock holding. It may have been a good company when you bought it, but its products and services grew outdated. Or its income statement got bloated with overhead. Or the rising prices of raw materials comprising its cost of goods sold couldn't be passed on in the prices of finished goods, so gross margins got squeezed to nothing. Or labor unions grew inflexible on wage and salary concessions when it was laid bare that the CEO last year made $200 million in salary, benefits, bonuses, and option exercises—even though the company's stock languished and shareholders saw negative returns on their investment. Most certainly, there are risks to holding individual stocks of even good companies.

The financial services industry has an answer: *diversification*. It is usually achieved by constructing a portfolio of several different stocks operating in different industries like, say, you might get with a mutual fund.

You don't get much better diversified than the S&P 500, so many investment professionals tout the S&P's long-term performance as evidence that buy and hold works, often citing Ibbotson's study of the performance of large cap stocks.

But is the performance of our stock market "averages" or indexes really a good way to measure the wisdom of a buy-and-hold strategy, even diversified? Are the performances of those averages or indexes valid evidence of buy and hold? Or are they really "a big con," as one observer (a subscriber to *Telechart Platinum*, a market data and technical analysis charting service) put it in his published note in the summer of 2005.

Building on that observer's cynicism, *I'm going to show you evidence that the market averages are not necessarily a good barometer of general business health, as advertised.* Certainly they are anything but buy and hold *because they are really actively managed portfolios.*

Let's first look at a narrower, but popular index, the Dow Jones Industrial Average (DJIA). It was often referred to by our grandfathers as *the Market.* Introduced in May 1896, Charles Dow decided that the investing public needed a simple way to look at the overall stock market. He compared the stock market to watching the ocean tide when you looked at the ebb and flow of the market's trend. One guesses that a primary motivation in constructing this tool was to attract readers to his fledgling investment newsletter, *The Wall Street Journal*. At the time, the *WSJ* was four pages in length and cost two cents per issue!

Those were wild times in the U.S. stock market, the domain of railroad "robber barons" and early-day Gordon Gekkos (remember Michael Douglas's character in the movie, *Wall Street*?) who would acquire, then tear apart companies, sell off pieces, and manipulate share prices.

Most investors in the 1890s actually preferred bonds, historians say, because they were backed by hard assets like land, factories, and machinery, and their interest coupons paid a more predictable investment return than stocks. An article at the Dow Jones Indexes web site (www.djindexes.com) about the Dow Jones Industrial Average says, "In 1896, investing in the stock market was considered a highly speculative activity, particularly with regards to industrial stocks. Railroad stocks were tolerable as they were the 'blue chips' of the day, but bonds were the truly prudent investment."

Dow's first attempt at tracking the stock market with an index of selected equities was in 1884, when he introduced an average of 11 stocks, mostly railroads. A relative few "industrial" (neither railroad nor utility companies) stocks traded, but it was not until 1896 with the introduction of Dow's industrial average that industrial stocks became widely followed.

The original Dow Industrials were comprised of 12 stocks and, by today's standards, not very glamorous names at that:

1. American Cotton Oil
2. American Sugar
3. American Tobacco
4. Chicago Gas
5. Distilling & Cattle Feeding
6. General Electric
7. Laclede Gas
8. National Lead
9. North American
10. Tennessee Coal & Iron

11. U.S. Leather (preferred)

12. U.S. Rubber

It did not take long for the shuffling of names in the Average to begin, according to the Dow Jones Indexes web site. (See Table 3.1.)

Distilling & Cattle Feeding became American Spirits Manufacturing and U.S. Cordage preferred shares replaced North American in 1886. Ten years later, Pacific Mail Steamship replaced U.S. Rubber and Standard Rope & Twine replaced U.S. Cordage. Then in 1898, Peoples Gas replaced Chicago Gas and U.S. Rubber replaced General Electric.

Just a year later, General Electric was brought back to the Dow Industrials, replacing Laclede Gas, and was joined by Continental Tobacco, Federal Steel, and American Steel & Wire replacing American Spirits Manufacturing, American Tobacco, and Standard Rope & Twine.

Is your head spinning yet? Especially in the industrial average constructed by Dow, the expulsion of names and their replacement by new members of the Average continues to present day. *By 1916*, an expanded list of 20 industrials, all common shares, substituted for the old list of 12.

TABLE 3.1   What Became of the Original Dow Industrials?

Company	What Became of It
American Cotton Oil	Distant ancestor of Bestfoods
American Sugar	Evolved into Amstar Holdings
American Tobacco	Broken up in 1911 antitrust action
Chicago Gas	Absorbed by Peoples Gas in 1897
Distilling & Cattle Feeding	Whiskey trust evolved into Millennium Chemical
General Electric	Still part of the Industrials (but not continuously)
Laclede Gas	Active, removed from DJIA in 1899
National Lead	Today's NL Industries, removed from DJIA in 1916
North American	Utility combine broken up in 1940s
Tennessee Coal & Iron	Absorbed by U.S. Steel in 1907
U.S. Leather (Preferred)	Dissolved in 1952
U.S. Rubber	Became Uniroyal, now part of Michelin

Source: www.djindexes.com.

National Lead, General Motors, Peoples Gas, and U.S. Steel preferred were dropped and 12 new companies were added. The list became:

1. American Beet Sugar
2. American Can
3. American Car & Foundry
4. American Locomotive
5. American Smelting
6. American Sugar
7. American Telephone & Telegraph
8. Anaconda Copper
9. Baldwin Locomotive
10. Central Leather
11. General Electric
12. Goodrich
13. Republic Iron & Steel
14. Studebaker
15. Texas Company
16. U.S. Rubber
17. U.S. Steel
18. Utah Copper
19. Westinghouse
20. Western Union

By 1928, participation in the stock market had broadened and the industrials had likewise gained in popularity. The people running the Dow averages figured that a broader average would better represent overall performance among the industrials, so the list was expanded to 30 stocks:

1. Allied Chemical
2. American Smelting
3. American Tobacco
4. Bethlehem Steel
5. General Electric
6. General Railway Signal
7. International Harvester
8. Mack Truck
9. North American
10. Postum
11. Sears Roebuck
12. Texas Corporation
13. Union Carbide
14. Victor Talking Machine
15. Woolworth
16. American Can
17. American Sugar
18. Atlantic Refining
19. Chrysler
20. General Motors
21. Goodrich
22. International Nickel
23. Nash Motors
24. Paramount Publix
25. Radio Corporation
26. Standard Oil of New Jersey
27. Texas Gulf Sulphur
28. U.S. Steel
29. Westinghouse Electric
30. Wright Aeronautical

The honest-to-God truth is: *The Dow Jones Industrial Average does nothing to support the notion of buy and hold. It is really an actively managed portfolio.* Stocks deemed unattractive or obsolete are periodically taken out of the DJIA, and replaced by others for how they reflect the growth and maturity of the U.S. economy.

Consider that *just from September 1985 to the summer of 2005, a full 60% of the stocks in the Dow Jones Industrial Average were replaced.* Some companies merged. Others fared so poorly in their business models that they no longer qualified for membership in a list of large cap leaders. So the Dow Jones selection committee found others that did. The *11 survivors from 1985* include:

1. Aluminum Co. of America
2. American Express
3. DuPont
4. Exxon (now Exxon Mobil)
5. General Electric (the only stock in DJI remaining from 1929 Crash)
6. General Motors
7. IBM
8. Merck
9. 3M (formerly Minnesota Mining & Mfg.)
10. Procter & Gamble
11. United Technologies Corporaton

The other 19 of 1985's Dow 30 are:

1. Allied Signal (merged into Honeywell and replaced by Honeywell in the DJIA in 2002)
2. American Can (became Primerica, replaced by J P Morgan in 1991)
3. AT&T (replaced by American International Group in 2004)
4. American Tobacco B (replaced by McDonald's in 1985)
5. Bethlehem Steel (replaced by Johnson & Johnson in 1997)
6. Chevron (replaced by Microsoft in 1999)
7. Eastman Kodak (replaced by Pfizer in 2004)

8. General Foods (replaced by Philip Morris in 1985)

9. Goodyear (replaced by Intel in 1999)

10. International Nickel (name changed to Inco, then replaced in DJIA by Boeing in 1987)

11. International Harvester (became Navistar, then replaced by Caterpillar in 1991)

12. International Paper (replaced by Verizon in 2004)

13. Owens Illinois (replaced by Coca-Cola in 1987)

14. Sears Roebuck (replaced by Home Depot in 1999)

15. Texaco (replaced by Hewlett Packard in 1997)

16. Union Carbide (replaced by SBC Communications in 1999)

17. U.S. Steel (became USX, then replaced by Walt Disney in 1991)

18. Westinghouse Electric (replaced by Travelers Group in 1997)

19. Woolworth (replaced by Wal-Mart in 1997)

How long before General Motors is replaced by Google or some other New America public company in the Dow Industrials? One is left to wonder about the value of the Dow if all of those companies that were replaced in the last 20 years had remained in this most famous of market barometers. Probably it would not be anywhere near today's value, although, ironically, some of the commodity-based and basic materials companies that were in the DJI in 1985, but have since been replaced, are doing quite well of late. International Paper, Chevron, Texaco, U.S. Steel, and Bethlehem Steel, for instance, are making a comeback with higher prices in forest products, oil, and steel.

At the beginning of 1985, the Dow Jones Industrial Average was approaching 1250. As we begin 2006, some 21 years later, the average is about 11,000, or nearly a tenfold increase. *Is that proof that buy and hold works?* Or does it instead prove that selectively removing and replacing portfolio components—an actively managed portfolio—works in earning decent investment returns? The Dow Jones Industrials' "rotating team of horses" ran a pretty good race through the years.

But if there is this much turnover in the 30 Dow Industrials' stocks, how about for a broader average, such as the Standard & Poor's 500 that is so widely used as the buy-and-hold crowd's benchmark? Well, *the S&P turns out to be an actively managed portfolio, too.*

A visit to the Standard & Poor's web site reveals that from 2000 to the early winter of 2005, the following changes occurred:

2000: 58 companies replaced
2001: 32 companies replaced
2002: 24 companies replaced
2003: 9 companies replaced
2004: 20 companies replaced
2005: 21 companies replaced

Is that a fair measure for evaluating the performance of a buy-and-hold strategy? In just the first six years of this decade, 32% of the world's most vaunted and benchmarked index was replaced, either because component companies were acquired or merged or because they simply no longer qualified for inclusion in a listing of the corporate elite.

Using the popular market averages as proof positive that a buy-and-hold strategy is smart and insightful is specious reasoning at best. The averages and indexes are not buy-and-hold portfolios. They are actively managed. Sometimes a company gets acquired by or merged with another, but usually a committee decides that one company has gone out of favor and no longer qualifies for membership, so must be removed and replaced by another company with better qualifications. And if you don't think it is an actively managed portfolio, just ask today's index funds, which are forced to periodically sell the stocks being dropped and then reposition the assets in the stocks of the companies replacing them—every time there is a change in the index composition.

Okay, the overall market explains as much as 90%+ of the performance of *any* well-diversified, long-only equity portfolio, however it is constructed. "Buy and hold" is largely a farce. At best it is a one-way ticket to mediocrity. Long-only active managers most often underperform the market averages because the only arrow in their respective quivers is to "buy good companies." And the investment marketplace suffers from overdiversification.

So how does an investor use these tidbits of knowledge to his advantage? More specifically, how does he get the overall market's direction to work *for* him, rather than against him? At the very least, how does someone invest in the stock market and realize its value-added *potential* in terms of risk *and* reward?

ACT II

IF ONLY YOU COULD...

In Act I, I offered where I think the financial services industry strayed from what should be its primary mission of earning superior investment results. The vast majority of industry professionals seem to be satisfied with being average, perhaps even *aiming* for mere mediocrity. The investment business is dominated by indexers or active equity managers who are little more than "closet indexers," and asset allocation "specialists"—all satisfied with inferior or, at best, average investment results because they aren't imaginative enough to figure out a better way. And we, the consumers, are asked to reward these professionals with premium compensation?

I cannot think of any other human endeavor in which professionals aspire to be mediocre. Collectively, we provide premium compensation to movie makers who touch our hearts, tickle our funny bones, make us cry, and win Oscars. We pay big salaries and bonuses to baseball players who can hit the ball out of the park 70 times a season, pitch no-hitters, steal 40 bases a year, or drive in 200 runs on their way to winning a World Series. Quarterbacks who throw more touchdown passes than interceptions and lead their teams to Super Bowl victories become million dollar bonus babies. We grease the wheels of NASCAR drivers for winning races—and they receive even more bonuses for winning "the Chase." Golfers aspire to be the next Tiger Woods or Jack Nicklaus (when was the last time you met even a club duffer who didn't want to beat his previous best score?).

We give high remuneration to wildcatters who find oil. We raise the pay of chief executive officers who stop the bleeding at a failing company and set the enterprise on a course toward profitability. Church ministers who attract increasing numbers of people to their congregation (to fill the offering plates) earn raises, too.

You get the picture. Why do we settle for investment goals aimed at just average or mediocre performance? And why do we pay big bucks to our professionals who achieve these less-than-stellar results?

For the traditional "I buy good companies" investor or portfolio manager, there are really only three ways for him to push investment performance toward truly superior outcomes.

First, he can concentrate assets in fewer stocks and do a better job of researching those companies. Such a portfolio is not as market dependent, so it has a lower R-Squared versus the S&P 500 or another benchmark average.

If you are pursuing such a concentration strategy, you are wise to set a target valuation for each company in which you invest. Then, when the target is achieved, *sell*! If a stock achieves what you have judged to be a rich fundamental valuation, then probability increases that the stock will not be able to earn investment returns at the same high rate in the future. Take your principal and profits, or at least a good chunk of them, and reallocate those recaptured assets into the *next* great undervalued idea(s).

For many professional portfolio managers, this is an impractical solution because of size and liquidity issues. They simply have too much money to deploy. If a manager with $1 billion under management is going to concentrate his assets in just a few companies, then those are going to have to be large or mega-cap names—where there are fewer overlooked opportunities—unless he intends to buy the whole company and take it off the public trading platform.

A *second* approach to investment excellence is to focus your "homework" on industry themes. Ask, "What is going on in the world?" "Are we finding more oil reserves and, if so, at what price oil is it economically feasible to extract those reserves?" "What alternative energy technologies will become economically viable and what companies will benefit when oil prices skyrocket?"

"Are interest rates likely to trend up or down, and what will be the effect on the housing market?" "What happens to steel and rubber prices with increasing competition from an increasingly industrialized China?" "What companies will benefit from a governmental push toward uniformity in electronic medical records?"

Answer these and similar questions accurately, consistently, and *early*, and you are well on your way to being the type of investor who earns superior investment results, much like Fidelity's William Danhoff or CGM's Ken Heebner (the Five-Star fund managers to whom we gave props in Chapter 1). They may not be right every time, but they understand that premium compensation should reward only value-added effort and generally above-average results. Sector concentration is, potentially, one such path.

The *third* strategic approach to achieving superlative returns is to put the single most important driver of portfolio performance, overall stock market direction, to work *for* you and diminish its work against you. Is the market likely to go up or go down? Is it "bottoming"? Is it "topping"? What is the likelihood that it will continue advancing to any meaningful degree without first having to suffer a significant, intermediate-term correction? Have you developed a system or timing model for establishing the *probability* of overall market direction in the future? If the overall market is the most important driver of portfolio performance, why the heck not?

The other two paths toward superior returns are important, but the rest of this book is about doing a better job of investing by using an overall market approach. Since the market is the single biggest factor in the performance of *any* well-diversified portfolio, it only makes sense that an investment strategy *using* market direction may earn correspondingly superior investment returns, even facilitating the better management of risk.

If you want only to achieve mediocrity, you don't have to go any further than Chapter 4, "Simple, Simon Says." My solutions begin with a simple discussion of how you can achieve mediocrity in a more cost-efficient way, perhaps, than what you are doing now. There is absolutely no reason to pay premium fees to a closet indexer or underperforming active manager for mediocre, if not inferior results.

But if you are really going to put the power of the market to work for you and avoid becoming its victim (in other words, earn better returns and better manage risk), you must understand various elements not just of asset allocation, but of market timing, too. So this section of the book, Act II, "If Only You Could . . . ," is primarily devoted to how you might use market-timing skills if only you had them.

After Simple Simon, I begin with some personal revelations about market timing, but then I offer some what-if scenarios: *If* an investor *could* time the Market, how might he put that knowledge and skill set to work in managing his portfolio?

Every solution that I discuss in these pages is most likely being done somewhere already, by somebody, to one degree or another. Little of what I reveal is revolutionary—except that most of the strategies are not broadly understood and are far from universal in their employment. Some of what I suggest will be controversial, especially among professional money managers. But if they stop and think about it, *everything* that I outline is doable. In fact, *if you have skills allowing you to better time the market, or access to someone who does, everything that I outline in these pages is practical.*

In Act III I will discuss some advanced concepts and strategies—and how I approach market timing disciplines. Act IV will focus specifically on my investment management solutions, applying my timing methods. Act V is an exposure to other people of whom I think highly, other timing methods, and even some other investment and trading approaches that are not dependent on market timing.

4

Simple, Simon Says

If you *don't* want to achieve superlative investment results and better manage risk, don't read any further than this chapter—but *please read this chapter*. If you don't aspire to earn better-than-average investment performance, you might as well not get overcharged for the privilege.

I had lunch a while back with a money manager friend of mine in California. He is a long-only manager, but hardly traditional, because he is already using some of the concepts and strategies discussed in this book and because he understands the importance of overall market direction on the performance of his portfolios.

He mentioned that he had just gotten a new client's stock portfolio, attracting it away from an old-line, underperforming New York firm. He said, "You know, this account is the epitome of what has gone wrong in our industry. The account is about $400,000 in size, and owns 80 stocks. On average, it looks like the previous portfolio manager invested $5,000 in each company, or about 1.25% of the portfolio's total value in each stock. And the stocks? It might as well have been the S&P 100," he laughed. The old manager was overdiversified; he was a closet indexer disguising himself as an active, long-only manager.

In Act I, I established that the overall market's direction explains as much as 90%—in some cases, almost 100%—of the performance of any well-diversified portfolio. Maybe more, maybe less; but only a handful of even "five-star" performers are among the active managers really earning their premium management fees. These five-star performers, like CGM's Heebner and Fidelity's Danhoff, are trying to add value to their clients' results and earn their fees by forecasting the industries that will outperform in the weeks, months, and even years ahead. In some cases, they are concentrating their investment assets on very few companies—but doing their homework thoroughly and with precision. The generously positive alphas they are awarded by the performance analytics firms are testimony to their value-added roles in client investment performance.

These value-added, long-only managers haven't sold out to the financial services industry's oversell of diversification. They have an idea. They develop the idea to a point of having conviction. Then they put their wallets behind their conviction. If they hit a home run (get onto a big industry trend or hot stock early in its development), their performance is going to be head and shoulders above the competition.

The sad reality, though, is that most investors, including most active managers, have become closet indexers. They overdiversify, usually because they have no special insight into emerging industry group strength or market direction. *All* that they aspire to do is to buy good companies. Managers advertise their abilities as better stock pickers to attract capital, but then they dilute that supposed talent with too-broad diversification.

If your only aspiration is to achieve a mediocre result, there is no reason for you to pay premium management fees to a closet indexer. If you get nothing else out of this book, get this: Pay high management fees only to someone who is doing something extraordinary, someone who is not settling for "just what the market is offering."

Moreover, if all you seek is mediocrity you don't need to pay commissions to a broker or mutual fund family for front-end loaded funds unless that's the way you are paying for other services he is providing. You don't need B shares, either, or any other classes of funds that carry extra high promotional expenses, unless you are using your broker as your "advisor." In that case, commissions are reasonable ways to pay for his hand-holding or mentoring services. But if you are making the decisions yourself, paying extra for B shares or loaded funds just doesn't make sense.

One of the investment industry's great champions of simplicity and low cost is the Vanguard family of mutual funds. Vanguard was the first fund company to offer an index fund (Vanguard Index 500) for individual investors, way back in 1976. It was a little ahead of its time, but certainly it was ready when the burgeoning interest in indexing accelerated in the 1980s.

If you want broad diversification and indexing, then one of Vanguard's many no-load index funds is just the ticket. While many long-only money managers (who are really closet indexers) are charging upwards of 1% in management fees per year to manage mediocrity, *Vanguard's average management fee on its funds is only 0.21% per year*, according to its web site in late February 2006.

With 21.5 million institutional and individual shareholder accounts and about $950 billion in assets under management among its 130 domestic and 40 international funds, including bond, variable annuity, and money market funds, Vanguard has created a great business catering to investors' broad collective yen for diversification. Your only decision is how adventurous you want to be in buying and holding a fund for the long term.

If you are going to be a buy-and-hold indexer, then the Vanguard Index 500 is an excellent way to put the long-term earnings potential of the overall stock market to work. If you want greater exposure to smaller growth companies, look no further than Vanguard's small cap funds. The sub-advisors to these funds are really smart and diligent at picking good companies. I've sold research to at least two of them at different times in my career.

Check *your* fund's Morningstar ratings. If its R-Squared is greater than 50% and the manager is giving you less than market average returns, you might want to reconsider why you are paying premium management fees to a manager who is doing so little to add value on your behalf. Use Ross Miller's (Miller Risk Advisors and the State University of New York at Albany) "active expense ratio" to find out what you are *really* paying for active management. I guarantee it won't be what the funds *advertise* as their expense ratio.

And if the fund's R-Squared versus the S&P 500 is over 90%, there is little probability that the manager's alpha will be meaningfully positive. He's a closet indexer, and you might as well be invested in the Vanguard 500 Index fund, Rydex OTC, or another low-cost, no-load index fund alternative. There are many. For the S&P 500 alone, there are index funds offered by such fund companies as Vanguard, Rydex, Schwab, E-Trade, Dreyfus, Fidelity, Mainstay, Scudder, State Farm, TIAA-CREF, UBS, and USAA, among others. There are hundreds more that may as well have the S&P 500 moniker attached, because they are constructed to perform like it (they just don't see any reason to pay Standard & Poor's a licensing fee for using their trademark!).

OR DO-IT-YOURSELF

Of course, you can also achieve investment mediocrity yourself. You don't need Vanguard or any other mutual fund family to get indexed returns, although the monthly, quarterly, or annual account statements may be worth paying those low management fees. All you really need is an online brokerage account with low trading commissions.

The exchange-traded fund (ETF) is one of the financial services industry's great inventions in the last 20 years. These derivative trading instruments are organized as trusts, priced to closely track an underlying market index or industry sector. They can trade at a slight discount or a modest premium to the market index on which they are based, depending on then-present market demand and supply, but the more actively traded ETFs feature significant liquidity and very little premium or discount. These include: SPDR 500 (Amex: SPY, based on the S&P 500 Stock Index); NASDAQ 100 Trust Series (NASDAQ: QQQQ, based on the NASDAQ 100 Stock Index); Diamonds Trust Series (Amex: DIA, based on the Dow Jones Industrial Average); and iShares Russell 2000 Index Fund (ARCA: IWM, based on the Russell 2000 Index), to name a few popular alternatives.

You buy and sell ETFs just like stocks. You can hold them in your online brokerage account, just like a stock, collecting any dividends paid. Depending on how much capital you have to invest initially and over time, accumulating an ownership stake in one of the indexes on a buy-and-hold basis is an inexpensive, cost-efficient ticket to achieving mediocrity. In fact, that's what a lot of the indexers are already doing—buying index ETFs. Even the closet indexers are "buying beta" in their portfolios by investing in ETFs.

Consider that a 1,000-share purchase of the QQQQ's at $41.45 in a Scottrade account is going to cost you a $7 commission for the $41,450 transaction. That commission is less than 1 penny per share, and less than one-thousandth of a percent of the assets being invested. In Grandpa's day, *he might have been charged 3% of the total amount invested as his commission, or as much as $1,242.50 versus your $7!*

If I were to pursue mediocrity and implement a buy-and-hold-the-index strategy, I would invest my initial principal over three months (dollar cost averaging), then buy additional shares on a regular basis as a sort of savings accumulation account. The value of my savings would fluctuate with the market, but over the really long term, say 20 years, I am likely to see a 5 to 11% compounded average annual rate of return on my money, which is the historical performance range of the market (depending on whose data you read), that is, as long as our market-driven, capitalistic system continues to thrive. If it doesn't, then I (and the rest of the world) probably have a lot more to worry about than the amount of investment returns I am getting.

To illustrate, if your initial commitment is to be $100,000, then divide your initial commitment into thirds. Buy $33,333 worth of say, Diamonds, on the first trading day of the next three months. All this is arbitrary, of course. It could be over six months. It could be quarterly. Maybe your investment day is the 20th of each month, or the 13th. Or you could decide to invest on the first three days on which the Dow Industrials are down by more than 50 points. It is all arbitrary.

The point is: to "dollar cost average" your initial commitment. Then try to make additional quarterly or monthly investments into the account, extending the dollar cost averaging concept. Over time, you will add to your total shares and aggregate asset value, with some purchases at higher prices, some at lower prices, but over time the portfolio should grow.

In Chapter 5, I will relate a story about *Dow 3000*, a book written in the early 1980s that discusses the *R-Factor*. The *reinvestment of earnings and dividends* causes the intrinsic value of successful companies to increase over time, and the share prices of those companies should eventually reflect their success. This concept is a cornerstone of the buy-and-hold philosophy and, too, the foundation of dollar cost averaging investments in an index. An index of good, successful companies should appreciate in value over the long term.

Remember also the lessons from Chapter 3: *The indexes are already actively managed portfolios* of good companies. The investment committees of Dow Jones, Standard & Poor's, Russell, and so forth remove the component stocks from their averages or indexes that no longer qualify or that get acquired, and replace them other, presumably better "good companies." You don't need to pay premium management fees to a closet indexer—or even to an active, long-only manager who consistently underperforms the market averages.

If you want to buy and hold the market and earn mediocre, market-average returns, you have only to decide whether you want a broadly diversified large cap portfolio, a broadly diversified mid-cap portfolio, or a broadly diversified small cap portfolio, or something blended—because there is an ETF to fit just about every investor taste bud. In Table 4.1, I provide a listing of the 26 exchange-traded funds (as of this writing) listed on the Amex, NYSE, or NASDAQ that are based on broad market indexes such as the Dow Jones Industrial Average, the S&P 500, or the Russell 2000.

TABLE 4.1 Broad Market Index-Based ETFs

Symbol	Name of ETF	Index Based On	Exchange Traded	February 3, 2006 Daily Volume
QQQQ	NASDAQ 100 Index Tracking Stock	NASDAQ 100	NASDAQ	121,104,000
SPY	SPDRs S&P 500 Trust Series	Standard & Poor's 500	Amex	86,042,500
IWM	iShares Russell 2000 Index Fund	Russell 2000 Index	Amex	42,793,60
DIA	DIAMONDS Trust Series	Dow Jones Industrial Average	Amex	5,109,400
MDY	SPDRs S&P Midcap Trust Series	S&P MidCap 400	Amex	1,759,100
IWV	iShares Russell 3000 Index Fund	Russell 3000 Index	Amex	886,000
IVV	iShares S&P 500 Index Fund	Standard & Poor's 500	NYSE	879,100
IJR	iShares S&P SmallCap 600 Index Fund	S&P SmallCap 600	NYSE	483,200
IJH	iShares S&P MidCap 400 Index Fund	S&P MidCap 400	NYSE	298,700
IWR	iShares Russell MidCap Index Fund	Russell MidCap Index	Amex	123,900
VO	Vanguard MidCap VIPERS	MSCI U.S. Mid Cap 450	Amex	90,600
OEF	iShares S&P 100 Index Fund	Standard & Poor's 100	NYSE	90,100
PZI	PowerShares Zacks Micro Cap Portfolio	Zacks Micro Cap Index	Amex	81,000
IWC	iShares Russell Microcap Index Fund	Russell MicrocapX Index	Amex	76,100
W	Vanguard Large Cap VIPERS	MSCI U.S. Prime Market 750 Index	Amex	72,300
IWB	iShares Russell 1000 Index Fund	Russell 1000 Index	Amex	68,900
VB	Vanguard Small Cap VIPERs	MSCI U.S. Small Cap 1750 Index	Amex	31,300
PWO	PowerShares Dynamic OTC Portfolio	Dynamic OTC Intellidex Index	Amex	27,900
ONEQ	Fidelity NASDAQ Composite Tracking Stock	NASDAQ Composite	NASDAQ	27,600
ISI	iShares S&P 1500 Index Fund	Standard & Poor's 1500	NYSE	24,200
ELR	streetTRACKS DJ Wilshire Large Cap	DJ Wilshire Large Cap Index	Amex	11,000
NYC	iShares NYSE Composite Index Fund	New York Composite Index	NYSE	4,200
FDM	First Trust Dow Jones Select MicroCap Index	DJ Select MicroCap Index	Amex	3,000
NY	iShares NYSE 100 Index Fund	NYSE U.S. 100 Index	NYSE	100
EMM	streetTRACKS DJ Wilshire Mid Cap	DJ Wilshire Mid Cap Index	Amex	—
DSC	streetTRACKS DJ Wilshire Small Cap	DJ Wilshire Small Cap Index	Amex	—

In addition to these broad-based index ETFs, many of the fund sponsors also have sector, capitalization, or investment style-specific products (i.e., large cap value or large cap growth). Some web sites you might find useful in exploring the ETF world include:

General Information Sites

Securities Exchange Commission	http://www.sec.gov/answers/etf.htm
Morningstar	http://www.morningstar.com
Smart Money	http://smartmoney.com
Yahoo!	http://finance.yahoo.com
ETFConnect	http://www.etfconnect.com
NASDAQ	http://quotes.nasdaq.com/asp/ investmentproducts.asp
New York Stock Exchange	http://www.nyse.com
American Stock Exchange	http://www.amex.com

Major ETF Sponsor Sites

Vanguard	http://flagship2.vanguard.com/ VGApp/hnw/FundsVIPER?gh_sec=n
State Street Global Advisors	http://advisors.ssga.com/etf/index.jsp
Barclays	http://www.ishares.com
Merrill Lynch	http://askmerrill.ml.com/publish/ marketing_centers/products/inv015 _HOLDRSSM/
Powershares	http://www.powershares.com/
Rydex	http://www.rydexfunds.com
Bank of New York	http://www.bankofny.com/html pages/sss_fse.htm
First Trust Advisors	http://www.ftportfolios.com/retail/ etf/etfsummary.aspx?Ticker=FDM

Okay, your potential pursuit of house mediocrity is out of the way. There are some great ETFs and open-end, no-load index funds out there, offered by some very fine companies with which you can put the market to work on a buy-and-hold basis, so you can be just average. But *the rest of this book is about achieving superior investment returns, even while more effectively managing risk.*

5

Epiphany

We have but very few seminal moments in our lifetimes. For many, these experiences are religious. For others, these awakenings help define our professional careers. They are times when everything begins to make sense. Such occasions not only open our eyes and ears, they launch us into a whole new phase of life discoveries. I was lucky enough to have had two such moments early in my stock market career. And they happened within about a year of each other.

EPIPHANY I: BOOK BONANZA

It was 1982. Directly below my office in La Jolla, California, and across the street from the historic La Valencia Hotel, on Prospect Street, the Old World Bookstore anchored a quaint, two-story collection of shops and offices. Mostly, the bookstore catered to the many tourists that flock to La Jolla year-round, from around the world. The shop featured travelogues, children's books, glossy "coffee table" art and history collections, and a sprinkling of general-interest titles.

From time to time, the store had closeout sales of severely discounted books. These stacks were usually an odd assortment of titles of which too many had been ordered or, more frequently, that nobody had cared to buy. It was in this store, at one of these stacks, that I experienced a stock market awakening.

But let's set the stage and put this moment in perspective. Some of my readers will be too young to remember this awkward time in world financial history. Perhaps they have read about the late 1970s and the early 1980s (when the market didn't always go up) in their business and economics classes. (See Figure 5.1.)

On January 8, 1973, the Dow Jones Industrial Average peaked at 1067, less than 10% of its 11,000 value as I write these pages in early 2006. What followed the 1973 market peak was one of the most vicious, secular bear market declines in history. Within two years, the DJIA chopped its valuation almost in half, touching bottom at 573 on October 4, 1974. Over the ensuing 24 months, it staged a terrific, 79% recovery

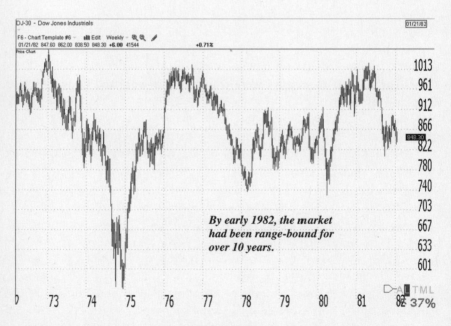

FIGURE 5.1   Epiphany—A Market Going Nowhere, Slowly

Source: Chart courtesy of Worden Brothers, Inc., *Telechart Platinum*. For more information, please go to www.wataugamgt.com and click on the hyperlink to TCNet.

rally (to 1026, approaching its all-time high). Then it struggled and fell back. A full nine years after the 1973 zenith, the Dow Jones Industrial Average was opening 1982 *still* under 1000, at 875—and continued to flounder as I browsed the closeout stacks of the Old World Bookstore.

It was midway through Ronald Reagan's first presidential term. Investor morale was at historically low levels. Professional portfolio managers and individual investors alike still reeled from the effects of skyrocketing interest rates, increasing federal budget deficits, high inflation, and recession. Stockbrokers were the brunt of more jokes than ambulance-chasing attorneys.

It was in this less-than-ideal business environment that I found myself in the bookstore one Saturday afternoon. The closeout tables were populated with titles that hadn't caught on, but I figured it was worth a couple of minutes to possibly find a birthday gift for a friend.

Soon my eyes fixed on an audacious title, *Dow 3000*. *Whhhaaaaatttt?* But that's almost three times the value of the Dow Industrials today, I marveled. A look inside and I saw that it was published only recently, in 1982 by Wyndham Press, and authored by Thomas Blamer and Richard Shulman. But Dow *3,000?*

Let's see. . . . America had given up on stocks, the Dow Industrials had been unable to surpass the all-time highs (barely 1050) made a full nine years earlier, and these guys were trumpeting a wannabe Dow at 3,000? No wonder their book had found the closeout stacks, and not even six months had passed since the book's release. Were the authors insane, or delusional?

By the time I found it, *Dow 3000* was marked down from $19.95 to $4.95. The manager told me it had been the store's only copy, the antithesis of a bestseller, I reasoned. So, ever the bargain hunter, I agreed to take it off his hands for $3. It would be a good conversation piece back at the office—and my friends across the border in Tijuana's mercados would be proud of my haggling skills!

But a funny thing happened on the way to *Dow 3000* collecting dust on my coffee table. I read the book and I became intrigued. I opened my mind and let the authors' thoughts sink in. It may or may not have been the greatest academic piece ever researched and written about the stock market. That doesn't matter. I bought into, internalized and, in my own primitive way, maybe even expanded on the authors' basic precepts.

Indeed, it is Mr. Blamer and Mr. Shulman that I credit for pushing me toward two steadfast beliefs: *First*, having an ownership stake in companies that we do business with every day makes sense, if done intelligently. *Second*, if you believe in the long-term viability of America's market-driven economy, you can't help but believe that the very *long-term* direction of the overall stock market averages is *up*. In fact, reading *Dow 3000* had me thinking that buy-and-hold *might* be a meritorious strategy after all!

The collective share valuations of U.S. companies in the past 23 years have far exceeded Dow 3,000, to be sure, so is this ancient history? No, because the book's underlying themes about corporate valuation are still relevant today, especially if the Standard & Poor's and Dow Jones investment committees keep throwing out the underperforming companies out of their averages and replacing them with the more successful.

I encourage students of the stock market to revisit the pages of *Dow 3000*. I couldn't find it on Amazon.com, so it is probably out of print. I couldn't even find an old copy for sale on e-Bay. So you may have to go to an antique book store, or the dusty archives of a public library. As I am writing this, I have found one used copy advertised at www.abebooks.com, for just $1.00. So much for my theory that the book might someday become a collector's item if the market ever made it to 3,000! Even so, my copy is not for sale.

Businesses that make and distribute the things that we buy, from toothpaste to coffee to computers to automobiles, assuming reasonably competent management skills, are going to succeed—precisely because we, and others like us, need and want their products and services. Sure there will be some failures. Misguided or underfunded management teams will err in planning and judgment. They might neglect their new product pipeline. Maybe they will get complacent about quality. But those enterprises that thrive and survive, keeping on top of what we collectively demand, will undoubtedly and persistently grow.

The R Factor

In *Dow 3000*, Blamer and Shulman advanced two formulas that separately forecast a DJIA that was at least three times its then-current valuation within the ensuing seven years, by 1989. They missed their seven-year target by a few months. The Dow Industrials didn't reach 3,000 until July 1990!

What they called the Asset Formula is really based on the calculation: Shareholder's Equity = Assets − Liabilities. It quantifies a concept: that ultimately the price of a corporate share is determined by some calculated intrinsic valuation—a multiple of the *net equity* that the share represents.

It is really a very simple, common sense concept. In the book they called it the *R Factor*: the reinvestment of corporate earnings after the payment of taxes and the distribution of dividends. When *positive cash flow* is added to *shareholder's equity*, the intrinsic value of the ownership stake in a company increases. Over time, the compounding effect of such an on-going reinvestment of earnings is powerful, they concluded.

That was my first real lesson in stock market valuation. Eventually, the market will recognize (and then reflect with higher share prices) the rising intrinsic value of a successful company. But this one concept is so elegantly simple, and I offer that common sense is one of the first great strategies to try when aiming for investment success.

Once a person's passion for learning about *the market* is fired, he becomes open to (and usually exposes himself to) hundreds, maybe thousands of techniques, tools, strategies, and concepts. A major challenge is sifting through the morass, separating the wheat from the chaff, so to speak.

Over the very long-term, the overall stock market averages always (eventually) go up—as long as you believe in the fidelity and survivability of a capitalistic, market-driven system (and today the world is nearly free of the bondage we knew as Marxism, Socialism, and Communism). And in a capitalistic system, combined with modest inflation, well-managed companies are going to be successful. First and foremost, *the intrinsic values of successful companies increase over time with the reinvestment of profits after taxes and dividends* (the gospel according to Blamer and Shulman).

Second, and more cynically, the popular averages or indexes are actively managed portfolios—to make sure that the indexes' component stocks represent successful companies whose good business fortunes are likely to persist.

But before I grow deaf from hearing the buy-and-hold crowd pound their chests in glee over my apparent "conversion," I need to relate my second seminal moment. *If you must*, go ahead, buy the indexes or one of the actively managed, long-only mutual funds. Sit back, relax, and enjoy mediocrity. It is yours for the taking, almost as certain as Tiger Woods having a better than average chance of winning another "major" golf tournament.

To earn truly superlative returns *and* more effectively manage the risks assumed, you need a mindful perspective of the market's long-term direction (generally up)—but don't let it completely rule your investment behavior.

EPIPHANY II: "SELL EVERYTHING!"

I read somewhere recently that Joe Granville is now in his early eighties, living in Kansas City, Missouri. I have never met the man, although I would like to someday. Twenty-five years ago, in January 1981, he was an independent newsletter writer when he sent out a "Sell Everything!" message to his subscribers. Of course, nobody could keep their mouth shut for very long. When asked why they were selling all their stocks, subscribers replied "because Granville said. . . ." So word quickly got around. Within a scant few hours, Mr. Granville's bell-ringing alarm became a louder-than-a-bullhorn clarion clamor making headlines around the world.

The Dow Jones Industrial Average collapsed some 2.4% the day after Granville's missive, followed by a 1.5% drop the second day. For a market that had been range-bound for seven years, begrudgingly moving between 1020 and 740 since 1976, that was a lot of volatility. For those of us optimists who believed in the long-term growth prospects of a free-market economy, those two days of free-fall were among the most disheartening of our respective professional careers.

I came away from the experience with one important question and one important observation: How can anyone be that right about the market? *And*, getting the overall market direction right may be the ticket to higher returns and better risk management.

Most of us are taught in business school, in stockbroker training, on television, or in mutual fund seminars, that *nobody* can time the stock market. It's ethereal. It's a noble cause, but elusive. On its web site, the asset allocation consulting firm Ibbotson & Associates has an educational slideshow asserting that asset allocation is responsible for over 90% of investment returns over the long-term and, *they say*, market timing might add a little over 1%. So why even bother?

So this cynical view of market timing is going through my head as I witness Granville's sell signal, but I am left pondering, "How can anyone be that *right* about the market's short-to-intermediate-term direction?" Of course, so devastating was the "Sell Everything!" message to prices in such a short period of time, many other frustrated investors were asking, "Is Granville's influence on the market *legal*?"

In Figure 5.2, a weekly bar chart of the Dow Industrials in 1981, you can see the sharp pullback after Mr. Granville's blunt warning. Most of the *short-term* damage was done in the two weeks after his published signal.

FIGURE 5.2 Granville's Market Call Effect: 10% Drop over Five Weeks

Source: Chart courtesy of Worden Brothers, Inc., *Telechart Platinum.* For more information, please go to www.wataugamgt.com and click on the hyperlink to TCNet.

In Figure 5.3, we see that the Market followed an initial 5-week decline by staging a vigorous, "In your face, Joe!" advance, to 1031 in the DJIA. *But even though the Dow Industrials went to new recovery highs, Mr. Granville turned out to be decidedly prescient* when the Market went into a year-long, roughly 35% collapse, from its 1031 high in May of 1981, to a low of 770 in August of 1982. And it didn't seem to matter much what stocks or sectors you owned, they all came under pressure with the declining market. Indeed, the pickings were slim for profits on the upside. *In retrospect, Mr. Granville's market call was right on the money.*

So, after experiencing the Granville effect first hand, *I was struck by the profit potential*, the *power* no less, of *getting the overall market direction right in shorter and intermediate-term time frames.* If you can consistently identify market patterns in which equity prices are vulnerable to corrective phases, whether they are year-long harsh declines or six-month sideways consolidations, think how much more effective you might be in managing your portfolio, I thought. Such an investor should be able to

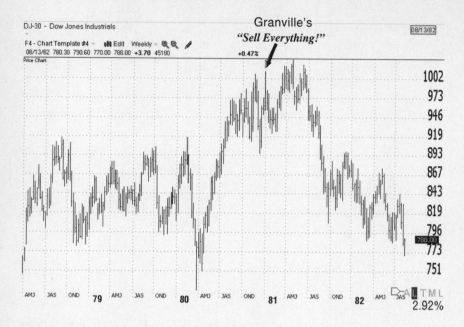

FIGURE 5.3 Granville's 35% Collapse
Source: Chart courtesy of Worden Brothers, Inc., *Telechart Platinum.* For more information, please go to www.wataugamgt.com and click on the hyperlink to TCNet.

more effectively manage overall market-related risk, as well as enhance the market's normally offered returns.

August 12, 1982's close would prove to be the springboard for one of history's greatest bull markets—and prove to be a buy-and-hold investor's seeming dream come true, especially if you had been lucky enough to buy at the bottom. In Figure 5.4, we see that in the long-term scheme of things, the 35% market collapse that Mr. Granville correctly identified was little more than the proverbial "tempest in a teapot." But *even during the 18-year bull market that ensued there were corrective periods of several weeks and months of which an investor could take profitable advantage if only he had a system for establishing the probability of market vulnerability, decline, or extended appreciation.*

Before 1981, I had never heard of Joe Granville, but apparently he had a good following. I understand that at one time he worked in New York with the old E.F. Hutton & Co., which in the 1980s had a clever

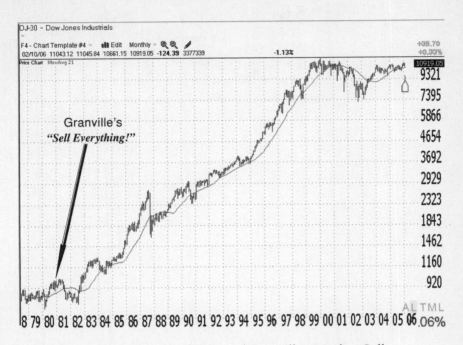

FIGURE 5.4 Long-Term Perspective of Granville's Market Call
Source: Chart courtesy of Worden Brothers, Inc., *Telechart Platinum*. For more information, please go to www.wataugamgt.com and click on the hyperlink to TCNet.

television advertisement themed, "When E.F. Hutton talks, people listen." Given his impact in 1981, I suspect Granville was Hutton's inspiration for the ad!

The harsh reality of stock market investing is that there are intervening fluctuations—downward—within the long-term uptrend. As I learned from Joe Granville, *these are return enhancement and risk management opportunities.* If you are like most people—what George Muzea ("The Magic T") calls "the trivial many"—you do not get enthused about stocks or mutual funds until the market indexes are near one of the intermediate-term or maybe even long-term highs. If you buy late, even pouring your hard-earned dollars into the best managed, Five-Star mutual funds, then you suffer mightily as stock prices (and the value of your investment assets) decline in an overall stock market correction lasting several weeks, maybe even several months—and you swear that you will never touch stocks or mutual funds again. As investors, our mission must be to become a part of the nontrivial, vital few, especially if we aim toward superior results, not mediocrity!

Mr. Granville opened my eyes to new possibilities for earning higher rates of investment return in the stock market: *Get the overall market direction right and you are on your way to higher returns, perhaps with less risk.* Right on, Joe.

6

What If?

So far in this book I have stated that:

1. The overall stock market's direction is the single most important driver in the performance of *any* well-diversified portfolio, however that portfolio is constructed.
2. "Buy and hold" is largely a farce and a one-way ticket to mediocrity.
3. Most traditional money managers historically underperform the market averages because of structural limitations, as well as some falsely based conceptual principles.
4. The financial services industry has oversold the concept of diversification, pushing investors toward the acceptance of mediocre performance.
5. Most traditional, long-only money managers are little more than closet indexers, undeserving of premium fee compensation even if they do advertise themselves as the best stock pickers around.
6. The managers deserving of premium compensation are either concentrating in a few stocks or timely industry sectors, or are much

more conscious of the overall market's direction and impact on their portfolios—and doing something about it.

7. New investment and trading vehicles, modern technology, lower transaction costs, and dramatic revisions in the tax code permit today's investor to achieve what his or her forbearers could not: better management of risk while earning higher-than-average returns.

What if there were ways to put the overall market direction to work *for* you, more effectively managing market risk *and* earning better-than-average returns? What if you *could* time the market, or at least establish the probability of market direction with 60%, 70%, or 80% accuracy?

How would you apply this knowledge?

Market timing skills can be applied in a number of different ways to fortuitous advantage. Before I show you how you might get into the *act* of market timing, let's consider first how you would use such knowledge.

There are *three basic ways* that market timing knowledge can be used to achieve moderate-risk investment objectives (we're not talking about CDs here; we're talking about the stock market):

1. *Buying the market/selling the market* by purchasing exchange-traded index funds (ETFs) at perceived market bottoms, selling the long positions at calculated market tops, and possibly selling short the ETFs at predicted market tops.

2. *Mutual fund timing* strategies, by transferring capital to equity index or stock funds at *buy* signals and then to money market to protect principal and previously earned profits—or to "inverse" funds that profit from declining markets on *sell* signals. Many of today's index funds are using ETFs to replicate the index, so they track the target index you are trying to time pretty closely. If you are permitted to switch in your traditional, non-index fund family, this is also a way to enhance the returns of your closet indexer or underperforming long-only manager.

3. *Portfolio enhancement and hedging* allows the nontraditional or alternative investor to increase the returns of a traditional long-only portfolio, or to at least neutralize the potential impact of adverse market conditions on the long-only portfolio. *Importantly, these strategies can be implemented without having to commit additional capital, and without disrupting the profit potential of the long portfolio.*

BUYING/SELLING THE MARKET

Exchange-traded index funds (ETFs) are some of the best investment vehicles ever invented. There is no time premium or discount with which to be concerned using ETFs as there is in index futures' and options' prices, nor other *intangible* contributions to price, like in options. When it comes to share valuation at any given moment in time, you don't have to worry about how much volatility there is in the underlying stock or index, or how much the option contract is in or out of the money, or if they split the stock at some time causing this or that class of options contract to represent more than the standard 100 shares. You don't have to worry about the "erosion of time value" with ETFs.

ETFs not only permit investors big and small to easily "index" the market, but they also allow an investor to take advantage of *market timing* skills and methodologies. You can buy the market or sell it short with equal ease. Are the Dow Jones Industrial Average's 30 blue-chip stocks a best match for your perception of the overall stock market? Then the Diamonds (Amex ticker symbol: DIA) are your best friend. It is a trust invested only in the 30 stocks of the Dow Industrials.

If you prefer a little broader market average of large cap stocks, then the Spyders (Amex ticker: SPY), based on the Standard & Poor's 500, will help you weave your investment web. Do you want a little more growth and technology in your portfolio? Then buy the QQQQs (NASDAQ: QQQQ), based on the NASDAQ 100 Index.

As this book is being written, there are 222 ETFs being traded on U.S stock exchanges, according to Worden Brothers, Inc.'s *TeleChart Platinum* quotation and market charting service. Many are industry specific, so in Table 4.1 I pulled out the most common broad market ETFs being traded today. Go back to Chapter 4 and revisit that list. I have arbitrarily ranked them according to their trading volume on February 3, 2006.

As with anything, the more capital you are investing in the market, the more important is liquidity, although it is less so with ETFs because, by charter, they closely track the minute-to-minute prices of the underlying indexes. If they get too far out of line by trading at a discount or premium, then the market makers have a financial incentive to take advantage of these price discrepancies via arbitrage strategies.

So, *if* you can time the market, one of the ETFs on my list in Chapter 4 may be your ticket to paradise. You'll be in good company, since some of the index funds being offered by the mutual fund companies (and even more of the closet indexers) are invested in ETFs, not really directly owning the stocks comprising the index. They get the same dividends as owning the individual company shares outright, and the tiny little sliver of management fee charged by the trust is more than offset by the advisor companies' own reduced management overhead.

MUTUAL FUND TIMING STRATEGIES

In 1984, the mutual fund division of Kemper Insurance rolled out a new mutual fund family called, *Kemper Investment Portfolios*. It was one of the first "B" share offerings, and Kemper distributed the funds through broker dealers. Initially, the fund family consisted of an *Equity Portfolio*, a *Government Bond Portfolio*, and a *Money Market Portfolio*. There were some interesting features, like the B shares' no upfront commissions paid by the fund investor, a declining *deferred* sales charge, and a commission paid immediately by Kemper to the brokerage firm that sold the investment to the client. At first glance, B shares were an attractive offering by the brokerage community to compete with the surging interest in no-load funds.

But the real novelty was that Kemper and the *Investment Portfolios* fund family facilitated *capital transfers*, or *switches*, between funds. Think the stock market is going up? Switch to *Equity*. Think interest rates are going down? Profit by moving your capital to *Government Bonds*. Don't have a clue, but think the market is vulnerable? Switch to *Money Market*.

My hat is off to Kemper, because it was one of the first fund companies to put the power of the computer to work for the little guy. Dick Fabian, the longtime editor and founder of the *Telephone Switch Newsletter*, had already begun to sell his market timing signals to subscribers by 1984. I suspect most of his subscribers were invested in no-load funds that permitted telephone exchanges. But until fund companies like Kemper began to offer services that took business advantage of the growing interest in fund switching, with free fund transfers, I heard that many mutual fund investors paid $5 to $100 in fees per fund transfer, if they were even allowed to switch.

Today, mutual fund timing has become big business. The National Association of Active Investment Managers (NAAIM), formerly known as the Society of Asset Allocators and Fund Timers (SAAFTI), headquartered in Littleton, Colorado, was formed as a nonprofit organization in 1989. It is a professional organization of registered investment advisors who *believe in the active management of client assets to reduce the risk of declining markets and to enhance overall investment returns.*

Mutual Fund Timing = Market Timing

Through the years, I have been to more than 100 mutual fund seminars and sales workshops. I estimate that 100% of the presenting mutual fund wholesalers touted buying and holding equity mutual funds, even adding to them along the way, as the surest way to wealth accumulation.

In Grandpa's day, the vast majority of mutual fund investment companies did not allow repositioning of capital in a stock mutual fund account to the money market's safe haven if you feared a general market decline. They complained that investors "switching in and out" resulted in higher fund expenses, harming all investors in the fund. And, they said, having to keep some cash on hand to fund transfers and not be 100% fully invested in stocks negatively impacts the fund's investment performance. They would have also told you that their team of portfolio management professionals were your best route to risk management and enhanced returns. And of course they wanted your assets to stay invested in their fund so that they could collect your management fees!

Several years ago, the fund companies began to allow fund transfers because improving computer technology made it easier and cheaper—and because competitive factors mandated it. But it was a bitter pill to swallow, because fund transfers en masse makes their revenue stream from management fees less predictable.

Smoke and Mirrors

I don't know who thought of it first, but somebody in the traditional fund camp came up with a strategy to *encourage* buying and holding funds, and to *discourage* the practice of mutual fund timing. Numbers were crunched, concluding that between 1984 and 2000, the Standard & Poor's 500 earned an average annual return of a little more than 15%. Their analysis pointed out that if you had missed out (not been invested in the market) on *just the 10 best performing market days between 1984 and 2000 (there are about 4,000 trading days in 16 years) because you switched out of the market, then your average return would have been only 11.6%.*

On the surface, this "analysis" makes buying and holding a fund look pretty compelling. Why, that's almost a third better performance if only you hadn't missed those 10 good days! And it gets even more compelling, their studies say, because if you missed the 40 best days in the stock market during that period, your average annual return would have been less than 6%!

I have an ongoing, friendly debate with a good friend of mine about this. A broker for a major national firm, he often cites these "missing out on the good days" studies in his investment seminars and client presentations as compelling evidence that market timing is "bad" and buying and holding a fund is "good." Like the rest of the buy-and-hold crowd, he states quite unequivocally that in order to maximize your investment returns from the stock market, you have to stay invested in the market so you don't miss the good days. "Don't try to time the market," he *always* cautions.

Compelling evidence, you say? Their numbers are accurate, but the *logic is flawed because it assumes that the timing system used would always be out of the market on its 10 best days, but in the market on its 10 worst days!*

The NAAIM, with more than 200 member firms that collectively manage almost $15 billion, naturally *took offense to the mutual fund industry's flawed claims* and asked an obvious question: What would happen to returns if you missed the 10 *worst* days between 1984 and 2000 (missing the worst days is a primary mission for timers)? Answer: Your average annual return would have been almost 21% instead of the S&P's 15% when always invested. And how about if you missed the 40 worst days, what would the returns have been? Answer, according to NAAIM's study: a little more than 28%!

Is this *compelling evidence that you should time the market and try to miss the worst days*? Hardly; the logic is *equally flawed because it assumes that you are going to stay invested in all of the best and miss the worst!* It may be every market timer's pipedream to be long the market in all of the up days, and in money market (or even in short funds) on down days, but it is implausible, to be sure.

In search of a more realistic analysis of these hypotheticals, NAAIM's statistical study actually went a bit further. They concluded that if you missed the 10 best *and* the 10 worst days, your average annual return would have been 17.29% versus the S&P's 15.02%. If you missed the 40 best *and* the 40 worst days, then the average annual return increased to 17.83%—still better than the S&P.

Timing mutual fund investments implies that you reposition assets according to your perception of favorable and unfavorable market conditions and trends (we will examine my market timing approaches in Act III and other timing resources in Act V). Importantly, an increasing number of mutual fund alternatives exist to take advantage of timing methodologies. And if you don't want to develop your own timing skills to manage your nest egg, your alternatives are even broader because there are an increasing number of market timing professionals who will sell you their signals by subscription, or manage your capital with their timing methodologies as my firm, Watauga Equity Management, is doing. As with most professions, some are downright good, others are better sales professionals than good managers.

Some of today's most *successful and growing mutual fund families were created specifically to accommodate financial professionals and their investment clients*, providing them with the flexibility to respond to changing market conditions, as well as changing client investment goals.

In Watauga Equity Management's mutual fund asset allocation services, I use *Rydex Funds*, where I have been a customer since the late Skip Viragh left Rushmore Funds to launch Rydex Investments in 1993. Now headquartered in Rockville, Maryland, my friend Skip formed his fund family with a single equity fund, *Rydex Nova* (the industry's first leveraged "long" index fund, benchmarked to a 1.5× multiple of the S&P 500), and a money market fund.

Today, 13 years later, the Rydex fund family is comprised of 50 index, sector, and specialty funds. Assets under management among all of its funds are near $15 billion. Some of them are leveraged to provide enhanced returns from a good set of timing signals. Some of them are *inverse funds* (otherwise known as *short funds*) that allow investors to profit when they correctly forecast that an index will decline in value.

The other 3,000-pound gorilla in the fund timing industry is *ProFunds*, founded in Bethesda, Maryland, in 1997, by Chairman and Chief Executive Officer Michael Sapir, and President Louis Mayberg. Not coincidentally, Mr. Sapir was formerly a principal at Padco Advisors, Inc., advisor to the Rydex Funds, so he was not a newbie to the index fund marketplace when ProFunds was launched.

I have never been a customer of ProFunds, and probably never will be because I have had such a good experience with Rydex. But I have heard some similarly good things about ProFunds and its 51-fund family of funds. Similar to the Rydex Funds, ProFunds' product offerings range from traditional index and sector funds, to highly leveraged and inverse funds. A less robust offering of mostly index funds comes from Direxionfunds, a New York City–based family of 14 long, inverse, and ultraleveraged funds. Direxionfunds was originally founded as the Potomac Funds in 1997, according to its web site.

The most important thing I can say about ProFunds (or Direxion, for that matter), is that the sometimes fierce competition with Rydex since the late 1990s has continually pushed the firms to offer top-drawer funds and exceptional client services, and to continually innovate. For example, *Rydex and ProFunds now have mutual funds that will respectively benefit from a strengthening or weakening U.S. dollar*, a fund product that Grandpa would not have thought possible.

For the market timer, these fund families have exceptional offerings, whether you are a professional advisor or an individual investor. But special fund families like Rydex and ProFunds aside, market timers can achieve similar objectives using almost any mutual fund family that allows free transfers between its funds. Just go long an equity fund when you are forecasting the market to rise in value, and switch to a money market fund when you think the market is vulnerable or has very little remaining upside left without first having to go through a corrective period.

Market timing works with traditional funds, sometimes better and sometimes worse than index funds. I recall that in about 1986, when I was using the *Kemper Investment Portfolios* fund family, my family's and friends' accounts that I was managing did four times (4×) better than the *untimed* S&P 500's performance that year while the Equity Portfolio (untimed) slightly underperformed the S&P.

Then, in another year, when the Dow Industrials were about +21% for the year, my timed accounts could only muster about a 22% gain—in a year that the Equity Portfolio of Kemper Investment Portfolios, on its own, was only up +4%! My timing was obviously exceptional, but I could only match the overall market's performance because the fund I was using as my trading vehicle underperformed so badly.

Obviously, it helps to have a fund that performs reasonably as well as the market. Index funds, like the *Rydex family of index funds, were a godsend to timers because they eliminated this variable of potential underperformance*. In an index fund, if the S&P 500 and Dow Jones Industrial Average advance, your fund commitments to Rydex Nova and the Rydex Long Dynamic Dow-30 Fund are going to appreciate in value correspondingly, varying only to the extent that they are internally leveraged.

Markets "correct" in some combination of two basic ways: *either harsh price decline or an extended period of sideways consolidation*. If the market declines, or even crashes, *any* equity mutual fund is likely to suffer in value. If you correctly perceive that the market will trade sideways for a while, or that there is little, if any, remaining upside potential in the market relative to the assumption of risk by staying invested, then you might as well be earning money market interest because you earn little, if anything, from stocks during those periods. As we pointed out in Chapter 1, the performance of the equity fund you use is probably at least 50% explained by the overall market's direction, and maybe as high as 99%. So if the market is going down, there is at least a 50% probability that your long-only fund will decline, too.

One of the truly innovative contributions to alternative money management aimed at earning superior investment returns was the introduction of the "inverse" index fund. These funds appreciate in value as the market benchmarks on which they are based go down. Why? Because they are always *short* the stock market (or the index they are constructed to mimic). Even if Grandpa had market timing skills in his day, it would have been difficult for him to take advantage of perceived market declines except for selling short one or more individual stocks. He might have been right about the market's direction, but wrong about the horse he had chosen to ride backwards!

Inverse funds, whether based on the Dow Industrials, S&P 500, NASDAQ 100, or another benchmark index, eliminate that variable. They are made possible by the advanced mathematical models and computer technology introduced in the last 30 years, and they greatly benefit the investor or trader who wants to take advantage of broad market direction.

Remember, such mutual fund timing strategies work best in tax-deferred accounts, and they require an investment of time and energy to implement—just like when pursuing superior results in other human endeavors. The next section discusses some things you can do in traditional and nontraditional, long-only portfolios.

PORTFOLIO ENHANCEMENT AND HEDGING

I call the third way of applying market timing skills, *portfolio enhancement and hedging*. It is really a hybrid application, a cross between *buying/selling the market* and traditional active asset management. I will outline my specific strategies in Act IV, but discuss them more conceptually here. At their core, these strategies represent the convergence I see coming, bringing together the rigors of traditional, long-only investment management and the flexibility of hedge fund structures.

I spoke recently with a Boston-based portfolio manager, who estimates that only about 5% of traditional, long-only portfolio managers do anything other than "buy good companies." *But*, he said, *that percentage has about doubled in the last couple of years.* "More and more," he said, "I hear of alternative strategies being incorporated into long-only models. Traditional managers are finally waking up to the fact that there are things that can be done in their portfolios, and they have to do them if they are going to distinguish themselves from the competition and better compete for assets to manage."

The Best of Times and Timing

One way for a long-only investor or (hedge fund) manager to distinguish himself from the competition with a *market timing approach is to neutralize the potential adverse impact of an overall market decline*. The individual investor places his entire *unleveraged* long portfolio in a margin account, then uses the marginability of the long portfolio to execute matching short sales of index ETFs when a sell signal for the overall market is generated.

The long-only hedge fund manager can implement the same strategy, selling short any of the ETF funds that best match his portfolio from our list in Table 4.1. Of course, you have to find an important balance between *best fit* and liquidity. An ETF that trades only a small number of shares every day is probably not a good candidate for most hedge fund managers, no matter how well the targeted ETF might match a hedge fund's long portfolio.

Why, You Two-Timing, Two-Faced Hussy!

Traditional, long-only equity managers are unlikely to engage the above-described strategy because they probably don't hold their client portfolios in brokerage margin accounts. Most are held in custodial accounts at banks on a delivery vs. payment basis, unleveraged. How can these managers use market timing methods to add value to their work?

The obvious solution is to sell some stock and raise cash levels, but then he risks being accused of style drift—not being long stocks or funds. So there's more. When you get a sell signal for the overall market, raise some cash in your long portfolios, but then use it to buy (go long) an inverse fund based on one of the broad market averages. An inverse fund appreciates in value as the overall market declines.

I am aware of at least one West Coast manager already doing this, and his investment success relative to peers during the 2000-2003 bear market decline is testimony to its effectiveness. He bought *Rydex Ursa*, which goes up in value when the S&P 500 declines, in his advisory accounts held on a delivery-versus-payment (DVP) basis at two major banks. He could also have bought any one of the several other in-verse Rydex equity index funds focused on the Dow Industrials, S&P MidCap 400, Russell 2000, or NAS-DAQ 100. ProFunds and Direxion also have lineups of leveraged and nonleveraged index funds, including inverse funds.

Remember, the mandate of most traditional funds and investment advisors is to be long a portfolio of stocks, seeking above-average investment returns from equity investments. Up until the emergence of inverse index funds, about the only arrow in the managers' respective quivers to achieve an objective of above-average returns from equities was to "buy good companies." Positioning a portion of their managed assets by going long an inverse fund is a backhanded, but effective way of at least partially neutralizing the potentially harsh adverse effects of a severe overall market decline (but preserving most of their long-only positions).

One of the most important aspects of these strategies—using the marginability of a long portfolio to effect matching short sales of ETFs or the purchase of inverse funds in an otherwise long portfolio—is that *both strategies effectively neutralize all or some of the overall market's potential negative influence on the portfolio without cutting off the presumably significant upside potential of the long portfolio.*

Selling Short ETFs

Let's focus first on the *selling short of ETFs* for the hedge fund or individual investor. If you don't understand short selling, then I suggest you read up on that before tackling this material. A good starting place is the Investopedia web site, at the following web address: http://www.investopedia.com/university/shortselling/.

I will start with a few basics, each conceived with two primary objectives: (1) Increase the returns from the otherwise unleveraged, long-only equity portfolio without substantially increasing risk, and (2) better manage, if not *neutralize* the potentially adverse influence of a declining overall market on the portfolio's valuation.

The Basics

1. *Develop a long portfolio.* I don't care what your research method is, or even where you fit in the investment "style box." Value, Growth, Blend? It doesn't matter. Small Cap, Mid Cap, Large Cap? Core Growth? Momentum, Growth-at-a-Reasonable-Price? It simply doesn't matter. Just develop your well-diversified long portfolio as you see fit, according to your selection methods for buying good companies.

2. *Buy your stocks in a margin account, but fully paid for.* Don't leverage your stock portfolio when buying your stocks. We are developing a moderate, even conservative risk strategy here, not speculating. But the offsetting enhancement and hedging strategies we will execute must be done in a margin account—because you are going to use the marginability of the long portfolio to achieve your hedging and, where the added risk is suitable, potential enhancement objectives.

3. *Neutralize the potential effects of an adverse market environment.* Your stocks are held long in the account, and will continue to be held long until you decide that each individual company's future prospects are overvalued or less certain. But let's say that you, the market timer, have gotten a sell signal for the general market. You can neutralize the adverse effect that a prospective, overall market decline might have on your portfolio by *selling short an appropriate number of shares of an equity index ETF*, such as Diamonds, Spyders, or QQQQs, *to match the marginable portfolio value*. Keep the short position in the ETFs until you get a buy signal for the overall market. When that happens, then buy back the ETFs to cover your short position. If you were right about the market decline, you will pocket a profit on your ETFs' short position, which offsets some or all of any potential decline in your long portfolio. If you were wrong about the market decline, then you will cover the short sale of ETFs for a loss, but your long portfolio will probably have appreciated in value, too, so it is most likely a wash.

4. *Hedge your individual stocks.* This step is optional, but if you really think the market is going to get slammed and one or more of your individual stocks will crater in a selling avalanche, then you can double-hedge by not only neutralizing the market effect by selling short ETFs, but also *selling covered call options against your indi-*

vidual stocks. The risk, of course, is that your individual stocks will defy gravity (and the prospective adverse market conditions) and continue to advance, and the call options you sold will either get exercised (and so your stock will be called away, or sold, at the exercise price), or to keep your long position you will have to buy back the call options you have sold, possibly at a higher price. In this case, you will take a small loss on the options, but it is offset by a rising stock price. Moreover, you have captured the decaying time premium that was built into the options price when you established the covered call position.

5. *Enhance your portfolio returns I.* Again, this step is optional. Because it means you can enhance your portfolio's returns, it also means that you are assuming additional risk. But you can control the level of risk, or not engage it at all. At a perceived market bottom—when your timing system gets a buy signal—again *use the marginability of your long portfolio to sell equity index put options.* If the market goes up, the options you sold will decline in value. That means that you can repurchase them in the future and pocket the difference in profit, or (if they are out of the money puts at expiration) allow them to expire worthless and keep the whole thing.

6. *Enhance your portfolio returns II.* Once again, this step is optional because it entails *assuming additional risk.* When you get your buy signal for the overall market, use *all or part of the marginability of your long portfolio to add to the overall long exposure by buying equity index ETFs,* such as the SPY, DIA, or QQQQ. You have a *great deal of flexibility in how much leverage you want to introduce* to the portfolio. The more ETF shares you buy to go with your long portfolio, the more aggressively you are using leverage and, therefore, increasing risk. More than likely, you would do this instead of selling index put options as in step 5.

7. *Enhance your portfolio returns III.* If you have been right about an overall market decline, the ETFs that you sold short will be repurchased at a profit, leaving additional cash in the portfolio. In addition, any option premium you received for selling covered calls will also be added to cash. What do you do with the cash, now that you are back to a perceived bottom of the market at a buy signal? *Add more stock to the individual company positions in your long portfolio with which to participate in the next up-leg of the overall market.*

While these strategies require use of a margin account, *you need not put up any additional capital other than to purchase your initial long portfolio.* In fact, executed right, the only time you might have to put up additional capital is probably because something went very wrong in one of the stocks comprising your long portfolio, which would decrease the collateral value of the long portfolio being used to facilitate the selling short of the ETFs.

The worst thing that can happen after you sell index ETFs in your margin account is that the overall market continues to go up but the individual stocks in your portfolio decline in value severely. If that happens, you are likely to get a margin call, but remember the lessons from Chapter 1: the more your long portfolio is diversified, *the possibility of your long portfolio value and your ETFs (based on the overall market) going in different directions is greatly diminished.*

The *application of market timing knowledge and skill is pretty straightforward.* At predicted market bottoms, buy equity mutual funds or add to long stock portfolios. Leveraged positions in exchange-traded funds are a viable alternative for aggressive investors, where suitable.

At sell signals, simply liquidate some or all of the stock in your portfolio or, better yet, neutralize the overall market's prospectively adverse impact by selling an appropriate exchange-traded fund, like the SPY ("Spyders", based on the S&P 500); DIA ("Diamonds", based on the Dow Jones Industrial Average); or QQQQ ("Q's," based on the NASDAQ 100).

If you are *long a well-diversified portfolio for long-term capital appreciation objectives*, you can keep your portfolio *without cutting off the upside potential of your stocks by selling ETFs short against your long portfolio using the marginability of your long portfolio.* You don't even have to put up any more capital.

Academic purists say that you are not really hedging the portfolio; you are betting that the Dow Jones Industrial Average or another index represented by an ETF declines. That's true. But our mission is not to have a perfect hedge against the individual stock positions, because that would cut off their individual upside potential. Rather, our mission is to simply neutralize the impact of the overall market's direction on our portfolio of stocks. By *selling enough index ETFs to cover the market value of our portfolio*, instead of selling "covered call" options on the individual stocks, or selling stock "short against the box," we allow for one or more of the stocks in our "portfolio of good companies" to run counter the market averages' prospective decline.

A good example is Quality Systems, Inc. (NASDAQ: QSII), to which I was introduced in the autumn of 2001 by QSII's investor relations firm, CCG Investor Relations, based in Los Angeles. I loved the story, and it fit all of the selection criteria for the *Small Cap Growth & Value* research theme I was publishing at the time. Interestingly, the idea also matched some of the criteria for my *Discovery Equity Research* theme that was focused on companies with paradigm shift products and technologies.

When I first initiated research coverage on QSII in mid-October 2001, the overall market was about midway through its bear market decline, and the stock was trading at a split-adjusted price of approximately $5 per share. By the time the overall market's major corrective period had ended in March 2003, QSII shares were trading above $12, more than 100% higher! As I write this, it is trading at $75, a 1400% return in less than five years.

Had a manager sold the QSII stock at any time because he thought the market was going to decline severely (which it did), he would have missed this significant investment gain. Had the manager simply not purchased the stock because he feared a looming decline in the overall market, he would have similarly missed out. But by selling short an ETF, such as the SPYs or DIAs, he was allowed to buy (and hold) the QSII position with its significant and probable upside potential seen from my research, and still he could neutralize the effects of the overall market's decline on the performance of his portfolio.

Let's look at a few specific scenarios (Tables 6.1–6.3):

TABLE 6.1   Market Neutralization, Scenario 1

Hypothetical Scenario 1: John Q. Solution *Investment Style: Long Large Cap Stocks* *Dow Industrials Are at 10,913*	
Market Value at Time of Market Sell Signal	$250,000
Portfolio Value *Lost* if 25% Decline and *Do Nothing*	$ 62,500
Market Value of Marginable Stocks in Portfolio at Market Sell Signal	$250,000
Market Price of DIA at Time of Market Sell Signal	$ 109.13
Number of DIA Shares to Sell Short to Fully Neutralize Market Adversity	2,291
If the S&P Declines 25% to Next Buy Signal . . .	
Market Price of DIA at Time of Market Buy Signal (after 25% Decline)	$ 81.85
Buyback Value of DIA Position (after 25% Decline)	$187,500
Neutralization Profit to Reinvest	*$ 62,500*

SCENARIO 1   First, let's assume that John Q. Solution has a stock portfolio of 25 mostly large cap, blue-chip stocks. And he holds these stocks, like Procter & Gamble, Intel, Texas Instruments, Boeing, ChevronTexaco, etc., in his Scottrade margin account, but *unleveraged. They are fully paid for.*

Mr. Solution believes that these companies' shares will appreciate in value over the long term, because he and others like him use their products and services every day. As long as he *continues to believe in the American market-driven, capitalistic system*, Mr. Solution reasons that these companies should prosper. On their own, *unleveraged*, he expects them to earn the traditional rate of return on the S&P 500, or somewhere *between a 7% and a 15% average annual compounded rate of return over the next 20 years.* Certainly that is a better return than a bank certificate of deposit, so buy 'em and hold 'em, right?

Well, yes! But no! Mr. Solution also acquired some market timing insights along the way. The overall market has just advanced some 33%, he observes, and some of his timing indicators are flashing warning signs of an impending, intermediate-term correction. In fact, his timing system just flashed a *major sell* signal that could lead to as much as a 25% decline in the Dow Jones Industrial Average.

Now a 1981 vintage Joe Granville might have advised Mr. Solution to "Sell Everything!" But that isn't necessary in today's world. All he needs to do is *sell a sufficient number of shares in the Diamonds (Amex Symbol: DIA), the exchange-traded fund based on the Dow Industrials, to fully neutralize a prospectively declining market's impact on his long portfolio,* assuming he wants to keep these stocks for the long term.

His portfolio has grown to $250,000. Let's say the DIA exchange-traded fund is trading at $109.13 per share (its price at this writing on February 11, 2006). To fully neutralize the overall market's potential adverse impact, he would *simply sell short 2,291 shares* of the DIA—using the marginability of his long portfolio to sell the DIA short. *No extra money is required.* In fact, he probably won't even have to pay margin interest to use the marginability of the portfolio because the short sale will result in approximately $250,017 (less a $7.00 commission!) being credited to his account.

Does this perfectly hedge the portfolio? Not in the least, but that is not his objective. Remember, the overall market usually explains at least 50% and as much as 99% of the performance of *any* well-diversified portfolio, however it is selected, whoever the manager, and whatever the research style or market cap size. Mr. Solution is expecting a down market, so his only real objective is to *neutralize the effect of the overall market's adverse potential.* He achieves this with the *DIA short sale.* If the Dow Industrials suffer a 25% decline like he thinks, then he will repurchase the DIAs sometime in the future at $81.85 per share, or $187,518 (2,291 shares × $81.85). The $62,499 difference between the short sale and the repurchase stays in his account. It's his. His market timing acumen and insightful strategy earned it!

This is not rocket science. The academic purists say that Mr. Solution is pursuing two different investment strategies simultaneously, and not really hedging. The benefit, they would say, is that the strategies can have some offsetting effects, and they would be right. Mr. Solution's long portfolio may lose more than 25%, say 32%, so in that case the long portfolio would lose approximately $80,000 in its value, or more than the $62,499 in profit he earned from the DIA short sale. *But what if he was like most long-only managers and investors and hadn't neutralized the market's influence on his portfolio?* Well, he would be out $80,000 in portfolio value and would not have the $62,499 in offsetting, market-related profits to reinvest at the market lows!

Put another way, Mr. Solution's *market neutralization strategy means that his loss at the market lows* (if the long portfolio declines by 32% vs. the 25% for the Dow Industrials) would be *only $17,501, or just 22% of the loss he would have suffered without the market neutralization strategy.*

TABLE 6.2 Market Neutralization, Scenario 2

Hypothetical Scenario 2: Mrs. Carol Aggressive *Investment Style: Long Small Cap Stocks* *NASDAQ 100 Is at 4,096*	
Market Value of Portfolio at Time of Market Sell Signal	$125,000
Portfolio Value *Lost* if 75% Decline and *Do Nothing*	$ 93,750
Market Value of Marginable Stocks in Portfolio at Market Sell Signal	$110,000
Market Price of QQQQ at Time of Market Sell Signal	$ 40.96
Number of QQQQs to Sell Short to Neutralize Market Adversity	2,686
If the NASDAQ 100 Index Declines 75% to Next Buy Signal . . .	
Market Price of QQQQ at Time of Market Buy Signal (after 75% Decline)	$ 10.24
Buyback Value of QQQQ Position (after 75% Decline)	$ 27,500
Neutralization Profit to Reinvest	***$ 82,500***

SCENARIO 2   Mrs. Carol Aggressive owns a $125,000 portfolio of small cap, *aggressive growth stocks*. Each one of the 20 companies in her portfolio possesses a product or technology that represents a future "structural change" in the way we live and do business. Abiomed (NASDAQ: ABMD), for instance, is in clinical trials for a totally artificial replacement heart, with very little direct competition, addressing a huge potential market. MicroIslet (Amex: MII) is a biotech company with an exciting potential new therapy for reversing, if not curing Type 1 diabetes. Amerityre (OTCBB: AMTY) has invented a polyurethane technology with application to multiple tire solutions, including passenger cars, industrial trucks, and commercial trucks, to replace rubber. Bion Environmental Technology (OTCPK: BNET) is introducing its proprietary and patented technologies to the California dairy industry, to help solve the growing air and water pollution problems caused by concentrated amounts of animal waste being flushed from ever-larger dairies. Natural Gas Services (Amex: NGS) is helping natural gas producers extract more reserves from their wells, faster, with compressors at the wellhead. Quality Systems (NASDAQ: QSII) has healthcare information systems software that may well lead to a paperless doctor's office and better patient recordkeeping. The other companies feature similar disruptive technologies.

There is *no way on God's green Earth that Mrs. Aggressive wants to part with any of her stocks*, because she is excited about owning each one. In fact, she expects at least some of them to yield 1,000%+ capital appreciation in the next five years as they get further along in the commercialization phases of their respective businesses. But Mrs. Aggressive has also picked up some overall stock market timing skills, *and her system just issued a major sell signal*. Historical patterns suggest to her that *a secular bear market has begun,* and the overall market averages may suffer as much as a 50 to 70% price decline over the next two years. What does she do? A bear market is bound to adversely influence the valuation of at least some of the stocks in her portfolio, and maybe all of them.

Thankfully, *she doesn't have to "sell everything" to protect her capital. Instead, she will sell* QQQQ *exchange-traded fund shares* based on the NASDAQ 100 to neutralize the market's looming adversity. She has a small problem facing her, though, since a couple of her stocks, the ones traded on the OTC Bulletin Board and OTC Pink sheets (Amerityre and Bion Environmental, respectively) may not qualify to be used as collateral in a margin account. She does some quick research, and learns that only about $110,000 of her $125,000 portfolio value is marginable. So with the QQQQs trading at $40.96 per share, she sells 2,685 QQQQ shares (2,685

× $40.96 = $109,978) to neutralize as much of her long portfolio's valuation as she is permitted by margin regulations.

Especially when you begin to get into these small cap "story stocks," the ability to keep your long positions' potential upside unfettered is important—because younger, smaller companies tend to act more independent of the overall market direction. In Chapter 1, we pointed out that the lowest R-Squared statistics versus the S&P 500 were usually posted by small cap mutual funds. Whereas a larger funds like Fidelity Magellan or Growth Fund of America have as much as 99% of their performance explained by the Standard & Poor 500's direction (because they are really closet indexers), small cap R-Squared stats most often came in between 50 and 75%. The overall market is still a major influence, but simply not as much as with the large, mega-cap funds.

So selling the QQQQs against the portfolio neutralizes the negative effects to valuation that result from an overall market decline, but the stocks are left long, unhedged. We pointed out earlier that in the bear market that began in 2000, for example, and lasted into 2003, the shares of Quality Systems, one of the stocks in Mrs. Aggressive's hypothetical portfolio, saw nearly a 10-fold increase in value between 1999 and 2003. Had Mrs. Aggressive made a Granville-esque "Sell Everything!" decision, she would have missed out not only on that significant capital appreciation, but probably also on the nearly 700% *additional* rise in share value over the next two and a half years.

During the same time period, the QQQQs dropped from a high of $120 in early 2000, to a low near $20 by late 2002, roughly an 83% decline. Let's say that Mrs. Aggressive's market timing system didn't peg the exact highs and lows, though. Maybe her short QQQQ position only captured 60% of the market decline. That *still means that by neutralizing the overall market for part of the time, she earned $54,780 in profits* that she can use to add to her long stock positions when she closes out her short position, or maybe invest in some new companies with exciting technologies that she has unearthed along the way with her research.

With market timing and this strategy, *she neutralized the market's potential adverse influence* on her portfolio's valuation, *didn't cut off the potential upside of her individual stocks*, and *added cash to her account to be used in portfolio additions*—all without having to put up additional capital. What was her risk? Well, if the overall market had continued to rise, she would have been forced to buy back her QQQQs at a probable loss, but her long portfolio also probably appreciated during the generally rising market, so at least some of any QQQQ losses would probably be offset by the long portfolio's appreciation.

TABLE 6.3   Market Neutralization, Scenario 3

Hypothetical Scenario 3: Mod Squad Portfolio Management
Investment Style: Activist Shareholders, Large & Mid Cap Portfolio
S&P 500 Is at 1266.44

Market Value at Time of Market Sell Signal	$400,000,000
Portfolio Value *Lost* if 15% Decline and *Do Nothing*	$ 60,000,000
Portfolio Value *Lost* if 25% Decline and *Do Nothing*	$100,000,000
Market Value of Marginable Stocks in Portfolio at Market Sell Signal	$400,000,000
Market Price of SPYs at Time of Market Sell Signal	$ 126.64
Number of SPYs to Sell Short to Fully Neutralize Market Adversity	3,158,560
If the S&P Declines 15% to Next Buy Signal . . .	
Market Price of SPYs at Time of Market Buy Signal (after 15% Decline)	$107.64
Buyback Value of SPY Position (after 15% Decline)	$340,000,000
Neutralization Profit to Reinvest	**$ 60,000,000**
If the S&P Declines 25% to Next Buy Signal . . .	
Market Price of SPYs at Time of Market Buy Signal (after 15% Decline)	$ 94.98
Buyback Value of SPY Position (after 15% Decline)	$300,000,000
Neutralization Profit to Reinvest	**$100,000,000**

SCENARIO 3   Mod Squad Portfolio Management runs a $400 million hedge fund. The managers consider themselves activist shareholders, so they primarily invest in companies they feel can be influenced to make management decisions that maximize shareholder value. Because these ideas can take time to work out, they buy their stocks on an unleveraged basis.

They own *equity positions in 50 companies, mostly mid-cap value names*. But Mod Squad's chief investment strategist has also been studying market timing methodologies, and calculates that the dark clouds looming over the market horizon are ominous. He feels good about the undervalued stocks the firm owns, but realizes that for the next 12 months quarterly performance bonuses may be slim if the overall market goes into a tailspin.

What does he do? Well, all of the firm's stocks are marginable, so he fully neutralizes the long portfolio from a prospective general market downturn by *selling short 3.159 million shares* of the Spyders ETFs (Amex: SPY), near their current price of $126.64 per share, using the marginability of the long stock positions. Again, while this *neutralizes the market influence on his portfolio, the significant upside potential of the individual stocks in his long portfolio remains unhindered.*

Let's say the SPYs have lost 15% of their value when the chief investment officer gets his *next buy signal* for the market. The firm *covers its short position in the SPYs, pocketing $60 million in profits in the process.* Then it *uses those profits to buy additional shares in the companies it owns*, strengthening its ownership positions and influence on management.

As an option, since it is a proprietary trading fund and is permitted by its charter to engage in any trading strategy, at the buy signal the fund can increase its long exposure by using the long portfolio's marginability to *sell some put options on the SPY*. With the SPY shares trading at $126.64 per share, that means each put option contract (1 contract = 100 shares) represents approximately $12,664 in portfolio value. To potentially enhance the portfolio's total return with an accurate buy signal for the overall market direction, let's assume the Mod Squad fund wants to use a third of its overall value by selling some index puts.

If the long portfolio is still at $400 million, and Mod Squad has just pocketed $60 million in profits from the market neutralization strategy, then the hedge fund is now worth $460 million. To modestly expose the fund to additional risk, but still wanting to enhance profits during the next anticipated advance in the overall market, we will assume that the Mod Squad fund will take one-third ($153.18 million) of its overall value ($460 million), divide it by $12,664 (the then-current relative cash value of the underlying S&P 500 index for 100 shares, or one SPY option contract), and so sell approximately 12,100 put option contracts. If the put option contracts (at-the-money) with two months before expiration are trading at $2.25 ($225 per contract), then that means the fund would receive a little more than $2.72 million in option premium into its account. If the S&P 500 advances into May, as suggested by the market timing system's buy signal, then the options are likely to expire worthless.

What's the risk? If the overall market continues to decline, then Mod Squad's liability for the puts they sold increases proportionately. The options may have to be bought back at a loss. However, if Mod Squad's timing signals turn out to be right just 60% of the time, they will have significantly enhanced the prospective returns from its long-only, activist stock portfolio.

WHAT IF, INDEED

What if you had market timing skills? What if you had a system for avoiding some of the biggest market declines, or maybe even for *profiting* from a market correction? Clearly, whether you are an individual investor or a hedge fund manager running a proprietary investment and trading fund, timing methodologies can be put to good use.

For those who disdain market timing, I say, "Quit being a hypocrite." Buy low. Sell high. Earn profits. Every aspect of achieving those objectives implies that you make one or more timing decisions, whether you have a fundamental or technical orientation; whether you are a value, momentum, or growth investor; whether you manage your portfolio by committee or as an individual; whether you are a man or a woman; whether you invest in small caps or large caps. Timing is inherent to every investment decision, whether you do it actively as we suggest here, or passively through asset allocation strategies. The biggest question is: Why *not* put the power of the overall market to work for you and your well-diversified portfolio when it can be your most powerful ally as you aim for superior results?

MY APPROACH TO MARKET TIMING

Hypocrisy is a disease, a cancer that disfigures objective self-review and evaluation in all manner of human endeavors. Nowhere is it more malignant than in the investing process.

At its very core, everything about making an investment decision is about *timing*. Buy low. Sell high. Earn profits, or experience losses. Whether it is conscious or subconscious, intentional or unintentional, active or passive, the success or failure—and the *degree* of success or failure—in making an investment decision hinges on the *timing of the capital commitment*.

So many investors I have met through the years, professional and nonprofessional alike, have expressed disdain for the notion of timing. One says, with nose so high in the air that I suspect altitude sickness, "Oh, I am not into market timing. I am an asset allocation specialist."

Another will sneer piercingly at such a suggestion, indignantly defiant, "Valuation, my boy, that is the key. Buy good companies when no one else has yet seen the value proposition."

Implicit to all investment approaches is a timing effect. The portfolio manager who makes an investment decision based on valuation is making a bald timing judgment: This stock, *at this time because of this value proposition*, is a good investment. Moreover, the relative success or failure of the decision depends on the price at the time of his investment. If it is at a low valuation now, then presumably it will have a high valuation at the *time* he liquidates his investment.

WE THREE KINGS

Think about it.

In early 2006, three friends (all professional money managers) wanted to buy a yacht so they could go on fishing and pleasure trips in the Caribbean. The yacht was expensive, costing $5.84 million.

So these managers sold their personal investment stakes of 100,000 shares each in Intel Corporation (NASDAQ symbol: INTC) common stock. They each got the same price, $19.46, so they are putting equal amounts of $1,946,000 into their big recreational joint venture. But did they get the same return on their investment for owning Intel?

Well, of course not, because their respective individual returns depend on the *time* at which they made their initial investments.

The first partner, a "value investor," bought Intel in early 2003, at $19.46. He had seen the share price decline from its 2000 high over $75.81, and figured that the valuation of Intel near $19 was just too appealing when you considered its price-to-sales, EBITDA to enterprise value, P/E, and price-to-book value multiples. After all, the world depended on Intel and its computer chips.

But here, three years later, he had this great opportunity to join in the purchase of a yacht, his Intel investment hadn't done anything, and it was a source of ready cash. So by selling he broke even on an investment decision that was poorly timed either on the purchase or the sale, or maybe a little of both.

The second partner, a "growth at a reasonable price" investor, was a bit luckier. Back in 1991, he correctly assessed the burgeoning personal computer market and figured that Intel would be a big winner. He saw that by 1986 INTC shares had backed off their initial IPO enthusiasm, declining to under 50 cents (split adjusted) per share. By 1991, Intel's corporate performance was strong and the stock was making successive new highs. He bought shares of Intel at a split-adjusted price of just $1.65 per share. Now, 15 years later, he was reclaiming assets on which he had earned a very generous 17.88% compounded annual rate of return.

The third partner, an advocate of "buy-and-hold," correctly saw that Intel shares were fairly priced relative to other chipmakers and its own internal growth rate in 1999, when he bought at $41. Unfortunately, he did not foresee the "dot-bomb" bubble bursting, so did not sell near the $75 highs less than six months later. So here he is, almost seven years later, and he is taking about a 53% loss on the total investment, a compounded rate of return of about -10%. "Oh well," he thinks, "the losses will offset the tax liability from my recent sale of Exxon."

Each one of these very smart guys earned a different rate of return on the same investment vehicle, all because of the *timing* of their initial purchase. The rate of return is affected by the price paid for the initial Intel shares, as well as the amount of time that has passed since the purchase (see Figure PIII.1) and, of course, the timing of the sale.

Even passive investors, whether indexers or the asset allocation professionals who periodically rebalance portfolios to fit some risk profile,

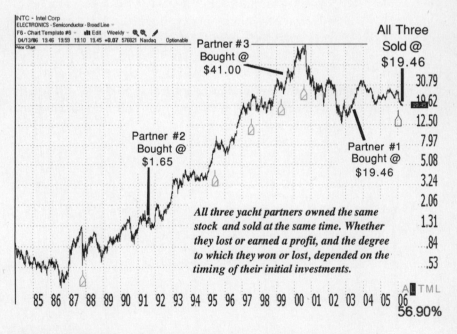

FIGURE PIII.1 Timing Is Key to Investment Performance
Source: Chart courtesy of Worden Brothers, Inc., *Telechart Platinum*. For more information, please go to www.wataugamgt.com and click on the hyperlink to TCNet.

are either victims or beneficiaries of time. For example, the buy-and-hold indexer who purchased the S&P 500 in late August 1987 at 337 has seen a little better than a 7% compounded annual return in the almost 19 years to March 2006. However, his counterpart who made the same buy-and-hold indexing decision less than six months later, buying the index at 221 in December 1987, has seen about a 10% return—same strategy, different *timing*, so different results!

Investors may have deluded themselves into thinking that *their* investment decisions are not about timing, but, like it or not, their results are subject to timing-related factors. Those who promote more passive approaches may *say* that market timing has very little to do with investment performance, but in actuality time and timing have *everything* to do with results. As with our example in the preceding paragraph, buying and holding an index fund over a 20-year period in 1985 yielded very different results than buying and holding an index fund over 20 years beginning in, say, January 1962. The passive indexing approach (using the S&P 500) between January 1985 and January 2005 would have earned a compounded annual growth rate (CAGR) of approximately 10.50%. Indexing during the period from January 1962 to January 1982 would have earned a paltry CAGR of just about 2.50%. Same strategy, same investment vehicle, different time.

Buy low. Sell high. Earn profits or sustain losses. And the rate of return by which you are judged depends on the *timing* of the investments and liquidations, whether you intended it or not.

7

A Timing Manifesto

Investment returns from the stocks of successful companies generally out-pace the rate of inflation over the long term. I opened Chapter 1 with this statement. It is offered by the financial services industry to promote "buy and hold" and the merits of stock ownership as a wealth accumulation vehicle. That implies, of course, that you have the skills to identify companies that not only have been successful, but that will be successful in the future, too.

If you hire an active manager, then you are assuming that the manager, in fact, possesses those skills. As you read earlier, if you have invested in an index fund you have hired a committee to do this evaluation work for you. They periodically toss out of the index less successful or failing companies (or ones that have been acquired) and replace them with the shares of other, presumably healthier companies.

I don't argue with the basic precept behind buying successful companies. In fact, I endorse it. The common stock of successful companies *should* out-pace the rate of inflation over the long term, if for no other reason than the reinvestment of corporate profits, after paying taxes and distributing dividends, increases a company's intrinsic value. As long as a company has growth opportunities in which to reinvest its profits, to make the company bigger, better, and stronger, the compounding effect of positive cash flow reinvestment—Blamer and Shulman's R Factor—over time is a powerful concept.

But our paths diverge when it comes to buy and hold versus a harsh reality: The stock market really does fluctuate. Buy and hold doesn't take advantage of these fluctuations. By not taking advantage of the fluctuations where probability can be established with some degree of certainty, buy and hold is a one-way ticket to very mediocre long-term investment returns. If achieving mediocrity is your mission, then why read this book? Probably, you intuitively know the truth: The stock market's very fluctuations facilitate potentially higher returns if we put them to work for us, and can even blunt the prospectively negative impact of market-related risk.

The market is volatile. It goes up, it goes down. Sometimes the overall market fluctuations work in the traditional investor's favor, but often they are adverse to his objectives for realizing positive investment returns.

For most investors, just like for the long-only professional managers, only *rising* overall market trends are beneficial to their interests. Downward trends put pressure on stock prices—nearly all individual stock prices, no matter how fundamentally successful a company might be.

There are, admittedly, industry sectors like precious metals or energy that may run counter to the overall market during any given time period, but they are more the exception than the rule. Usually, those exceptions are driven by industry-specific fundamentals: inflation run amok (gold), a hurricane wiping out nine gasoline refineries in the Gulf Coast (energy), or new federal regulations requiring uniform patient record-keeping (health-care information software).

Are overall market fluctuations necessary? Yes, because investors' collective emotions of Fear and Greed propel prices to *oversold* (extreme pessimism) and *overbought* (extreme optimism) valuation levels. Prices need periodic reality checks in both directions. *But is it necessary for portfolio valuations to suffer to the same extent as individual share prices?*

Not necessarily, and especially not in this day and age. This is where your putting to work the number-1 influence on diversified portfolio performance comes in handy. In Act II, I discussed conceptually potential portfolio management solutions that could be applied if only the investor or manager had market timing skills. Act III is about *my personal approach to market timing.* There are accounts of my discovery of key market timing principles, how I evolved toward market timing, and then what some of my timing signals look like.

Ultimately, the market's long-term trends reflect the expansions and contractions of the business cycle. That sounds simple enough, but it becomes a bit more complicated when you understand that the market *discounts* actual economic events and circumstances up to several weeks, even months in advance of their actual occurrence.

The challenge for anyone disdaining buy-and-hold investment philosophies (where you ride out any rough weather in the market, staying invested during the contractions as well as the expansion periods) is *how to time the overall market's fluctuations.* Are you a trend-follower? If so, then you generally wait until the next uptrend is *confirmed* before buying stocks or mutual funds. On the other end of the trend, you hold stocks until the next down-leg is firmly established before selling.

It is just my opinion, but *I regard buying late and selling late as the surest way to increase risk and diminish return potential.* Through the years I have listened to the philosophies of many investors, traders, and analysts. Many eschew "contrarian principles" in favor of trend-following methodologies. They say, "Nobody can pick the top or bottom," or "Don't try to catch a falling knife."

Of course there are elements of truth in these words of caution. However, those who utter them *fail to understand what makes the market go up and down.* Moreover, they are reluctant to admit any trend-following method's tragic flaw: its susceptibility to a *series* of small losses (plus extra transaction costs) during "whipsaw" or sideways consolidation phases. Every once in a while an established trend runs away to great profitability, whether up or down. But the *intervening whipsaw losses drag back the overall investment returns toward mediocrity.*

I prefer a contrarian approach to overall stock market timing for one simple reason: *Things are cheapest when no one else wants them.* Conversely, *they are the most expensive when everybody wants them.* This is as true with stocks as with anything else, whether you are talking about the valuation of real estate, gold bullion, rolls of steel, sports cars, baseball cards, or NASCAR collectibles.

In stock market investing, the trick is having research tools to accurately predict the *probability* of a top or bottom forming just prior to a major reversal in trend. The *good news* is that in addition to participating in more of the next primary trend, the *use of well-executed contrarian principles* also means that your entry decisions are *at lower risk levels,* whether you are buying long or selling short.

Other than the fact that your probability decision might be wrong or ill-timed, the biggest risk in using a contrarian-based model is time-related: At whatever great value point you identify a contrarian-based opportunity, sometimes it simply takes *time* for other people to recognize the value proposition of the opportunity—and for the company, sector, or broader market circumstances to realize their full valuation potential.

MARY, MARY, QUITE CONTRARY, HOW DOES YOUR GARDEN GROW?

Understanding contrarian thinking, though, is a fairly pragmatic exercise. First, the stock market ultimately reflects the expansions and contractions of the business and economic cycles, so it is going to go up and down with the changing fortunes of the publicly traded companies operating in our market-driven economic system.

But there is not a concurrent correlation between the changing fortunes of companies and their market prices, because the market *discounts* future business and economic conditions in advance of their occurrence. The market's very fluctuations are driven by Fear and Greed. Together, investors bid prices and stock valuations up because a majority of them (or those with the most buying power) are optimistic about the future. They want to profit from the expected economic expansion by owning shares in the companies that stand to benefit. So buy.

Conversely, stock prices go down because a majority of investors are pessimistic about the future and are afraid of losing money if they continue to own stocks. "Get me out of here," they say. So sell.

In both cases, *greed and fear tend to drive prices to unsustainable extremes*. What happens at these extremes? Whether institutions, exchange specialists, insiders, or individuals, "smart money" will *accumulate* value at extreme low prices and *distribute* value at extreme high prices. Buy low. Sell high. Earn profits.

In principle, this is pretty simple logic, right? Contrarian decision-making *anticipates* changes in a market's primary trends. Instead of giving up the first 20 to 30% of a major market advance (as you might with a trend-following approach), contrarian methods aim to buy closer to the bottom and sell closer to the top.

The trick is *ascertaining when smart money investors*—those buying near the bottom and selling near the top—*are really accumulating or distributing value*. Unfortunately, they don't put up billboards along either I-5 or I-95, nor do they run television ads during the Super Bowl telling everyone what they are doing. So it is not always an easy endeavor to figure out whether you are catching a falling knife or, say, a falling peacock feather.

I argue that *there is only marginal value to fundamental analysis in making effective, contrarian-based timing decisions.* Value investors might point to historically low multiples of stocks versus their reported financial results according to various indicators, like *price-to-earnings* or *enterprise value-to-EBITDA* ratios. But failing companies are likely to post earnings or EBITDA results that will disappoint investors—and bring those valuations back into line without the share price component moving even a little bit. In fact, after a company reports its disappointing financial results, what was once perceived as an undervalued equity may instead be judged overvalued!

A macrofundamental theorist may point to a period of low interest rates as being conducive to increased levels of business activity because of low capital financing costs. But a continuing slide in the economy could also prompt the monetary regulators to let interest rates go lower still while companies continue to be challenged in their respective financial performances.

A major problem is that most fundamentally derived corporate and economic information is dated. I admit that this has gotten better, in recent years, with regulatory reforms that reflect modern technology and communications processes. For example, the SEC has pushed for more, and more expedient, transparency in the disclosure of material information and what corporate insiders are doing with their shareholdings. In the late 1970s, insider transactions weren't required to be reported for two weeks after the transaction. Today, the SEC requires them to be reported the *second day* after the purchase or sale.

While the information is more useful than before, it is still reported late. Insider transactions are arguably the best reported fundamental information available. Still, anyone analyzing such fundamental data must accumulate data on all of the insider buys and sells and make a decision about whether there is more net buying or more net selling, then investigate the likely motivations of the buyers and sellers, which can be a time-consuming process. Is Mr. CEO selling because a new drug isn't going to get Food and Drug Administration approval, or is the insider transaction related to annual charitable gifts to the Boston Symphony, Children's Hospital, and the Blowing Rock (North Carolina) Community Arts Center?

The delay factor—first in reporting and then the time required to assimilate, analyze, and reach a conclusion—*is the major problem with almost all fundamental research*. At the end of a fiscal quarter, companies have as many as 45 days before they are required to report sales and earnings and still be compliant with SEC regulations. A lot can happen in that month and a half before the data is required to be available to the public for dissemination, analysis, and decision making. And all of that interim stuff happening between the end of a financial period and when it is reported often isn't reported until the *next* period results are disclosed.

A CONTRARIAN'S TOOLBOX

For making market timing decisions using contrarian principles, I turn to cyclical and technical analysis. I look for repeated historical patterns that establish the *probability* of whether a particular pattern will repeat itself in a then-current market environment.

There are so many different variables in market forecasting that it is no wonder most people give up, even saying it can't be done. I am the first to admit that forecasting market direction is not for everyone, and certainly it is not easy. There are few absolutes other than the certain knowledge that prices are likely to change. So determining the *probability* of future market direction is about the best (legal) goal that we can pursue. But if you are right more times than you are wrong, and when you are wrong have mechanisms in place to quickly identify your mortality, then *over the long run you can add value to investment returns so that they become much more than mediocre, even superior.*

8

Silencing Statistical Noise

Cycle theorists suggest that there is a natural rhythm to the seemingly random ebb and flow of the market's up and down gyrations. I was first introduced to cycle considerations in 1979, when a brokerage customer in San Diego invited me to his office to discuss "weather cycle" models that, he said, influenced commodity price movements. Of particular interest to him at the time was what he claimed to be a 400-year global weather cycle. The cycle was generally changing, he asserted, from "warmer and wetter" than average, to "colder and drier."

I can tell you that I didn't immediately throw away my umbrella and start carrying a fur-lined trench coat (not in San Diego, anyway!), but *I was intrigued and started thinking about cycles and their potential applications to the stock market.*

My ears perked up again in 1982, when another San Diego customer introduced me to his work on stock market cycles. I embarked on a mission to read as much about cycles as I could, or at least as much as my limited knowledge of mathematics would allow, to get a handle on the *practical* applications of cycle theory to the stock market.

I remember hearing one cycle theorist speak avidly on his hotline about a 10-day cycle's "topping" the next day. The next day I listened to

107

his hotline message and he revealed that a 13-week cycle interval was due to bottom, and this was a *really* important market event. Then, less than a week later the same analyst would talk about a 300-day cycle that was due to top within the next couple of days, and this was going to be a life-changing experience!

Every day, there was a different cycle coming due, some bottoming and some topping, and each one was more important than all previous ones. It was enough make your head spin! Of course, if you weren't also thinking about the *practical* application of cycles, there was an ever-increasing urgency to subscribe to hotlines and newsletters to find out when the next big market tsunami was going to hit!

As I became more aware of other people's work with cycles, I realized that, theoretically, there are arguably an *infinite number of different cycle intervals* impacting the market simultaneously. Some of these theoretical market influences are rising; some are declining. Some are topping, about to turn downward. Others are bottoming, about to exert upward pressure.

As a result of this perplexing realization, *I came to one of those defining moments in research*. I concluded that there was absolutely no *practical application* to cycle analysis, *unless* you somehow harness the *simultaneous* influences of several cycle intervals. But first you had to identify cycle intervals that individually had a discernable, important influence on the overall market's behavior and direction. And then you had to ascertain as best you could the calendar dates around which they bottomed, or even nested with other cycle intervals.

By this time, I was living in Chicago, trying to make a living in the commodity markets and coaching rugby. Through rugby, I became acquainted with a young graduate student at the University of Chicago, Jeffrey Heisler, who was working on an MBA in Finance. We started comparing theories and notes on the stock market, and Jeff ended up challenging me to a duel of sorts. For his Master's thesis in statistical decision making, he threw down the proverbial gauntlet—that he could devise a computer program that would do a better job of predicting market direction, *using my own indicators!*

In retrospect, this was *one of the most useful research exercises I have ever undertaken*. In order to give him a fair chance at winning, I had to quantify and clearly define every single indicator or market timing tool I was using. There could be absolutely no subjectivity.

Keep in mind that this was in 1985. Personal computers were not yet widespread fare in the business world. I had an old, agonizingly slow Apple II+, and it would be another two years before I graduated to an IBM DOS-based PC. I was *hand-calculating and graphing* approximately 40 indicators every day, *and* monitoring a set of about 15 individual cycle studies. If only Michael Dell could have come back from the future!

Our challenge ended in a virtual dead heat (OK, I won, but only by a little bit), but I was so impressed with Jeff's model that I took the results of his statistical study very seriously. Using multilinear regression and other statistical tools that were largely foreign to me, he determined that of the 40 calculations I was making daily, approximately 98% of the entire predictive value could be gleaned from just 8 of them. To quote Jeff at the time, "The rest are just statistical noise." And surprisingly, he said, the cycle studies represented a good chunk of that predictive value.

I am deeply indebted to Jeff. The time I spent doing calculations and analysis was cut by at least 80%—and the results included *more focused, more confident, and more accurate market timing decisions*. Moreover, in the process of quantifying all of my theoretical research models and indicators, we were able to toy with my long-held belief that multiple cycle intervals could be mathematically combined to a single, *net influence* cycle effect. In fact, according to Jeff's regression model, the "net influence" cycle model we created for this exercise was one of the *most* significant factors in the computer's predictive accuracy.

I am not going to share the individual cycle time intervals, nor the nesting dates around which the cycle intervals form near simultaneous bottoms. They took a lot of years and effort to acquire. These are powerful market timing tools and the markets are, ultimately, efficient. The more people know about them, then the less effective they become. But that doesn't mean that a stock market student can't be exposed to the conceptual approach—and figure out another cycle model that suits *his* personality, *his* perspective, *his* risk tolerance, and *his* investment objectives.

Of my 15 cycles monitored, we identified six cycle intervals that appeared to have some degree of predictive value, individually. They are graphically depicted in Figures 8.1 to 8.6, beginning with the shortest time interval.

Taken separately, there isn't really a rhyme or reason as to why the individual cycle studies should work as tools, at least very consistently. They bottom at different times. Sometimes two are rising while the others are declining. In fact, there is almost always a different combination of rising and declining individual intervals. Of what practical use is that?

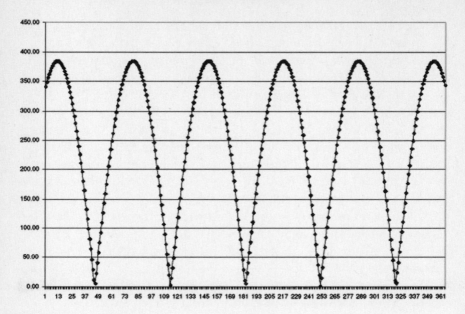

FIGURE 8.1   Cycle ST-10

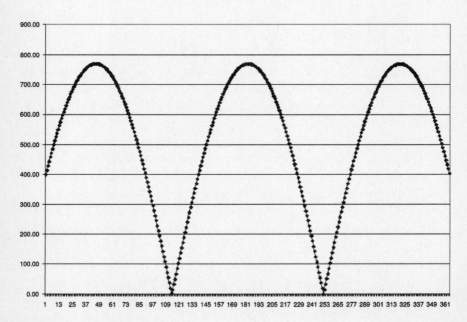

FIGURE 8.2   Cycle ST-20

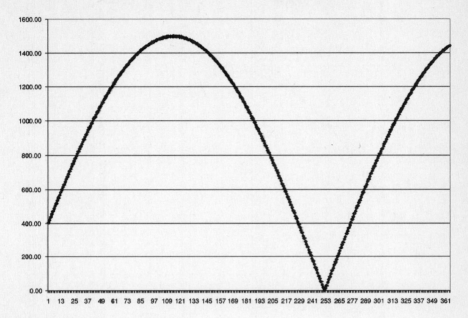

FIGURE 8.3   Cycle ST-30

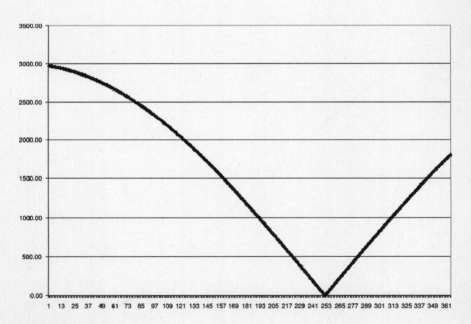

FIGURE 8.4   Cycle ST-40

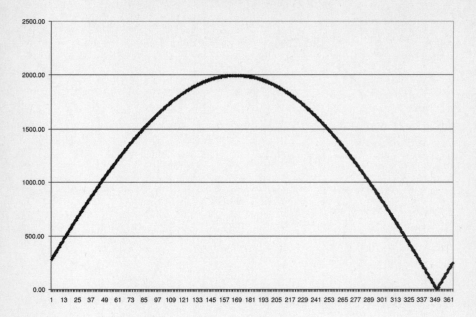

FIGURE 8.5　Cycle ST-50

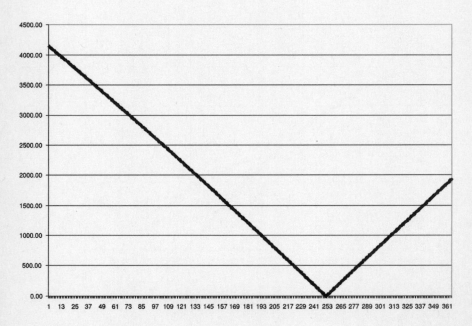

FIGURE 8.6　Cycle ST-60

I concluded that there was little consistently practical effect to using these individual cycle intervals. Sure, once in a while there were correlations with price bottoms, but there were enough misses that the correlations seemed to be coincidence.

But, with Jeff's help, we mathematically combined the six individual cycles, to create a net influence cycle effect. The resulting picture was startling, in and of itself. (See Figure 8.7.)

What was the first observation I made when I saw the graphical representation of this "net influence" model? While the individual component cycles all rise and fall at their own regular pace, *there is no longer any sort of uniformity in the picture when they are combined.* The tops and bottoms occur at different heights, and at irregular intervals. In a word, there is a *randomness to the pattern that has an extraordinary resemblance to the way the actual stock market fluctuates.*

So how can this be put to work? At any given point in time, this net influence cycle study offers us a *theoretical* direction for the market, presumably the direction that the overall market *should* be going. It also gives us calendar dates around which tops and bottoms *should* occur.

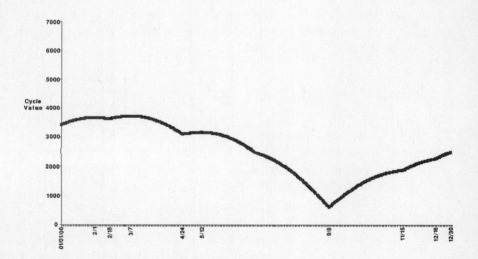

FIGURE 8.7   Net Influence Cycle Studies, 2006
Source: Wataugh Equity Management, using Microsoft Excel. Collaboration of David Rogers and Jeffrey Heisler.

Notice I have emphasized the words *should* and *theoretical* a couple of times. In applying this model to my market forecasting research for the last 20+ years, I have made a few determinations.

First, what is going on in the world dictates actual market direction. Remember my earlier thought, that ultimately the stock market's intermediate and longer-term trends reflect the contractions and expansions of the business cycle. Except for the occasional surprise (e.g., terrorist attack) or natural disaster (e.g., Hurricane Katrina), the market actually discounts, or foreshadows, actual economic events between three and nine months in advance of their occurrence. If the *theoretical*, net influence cycle indicator direction is down, then market prices may be trending down *or* they simply may not be going up as vigorously as they would if an *up cycle* was in effect.

Second, occasionally the market absolutely defies the theoretical direction of the indicator (usually to the upside). There appears, however, to be a relationship between these times and the absolute value of the theoretical indicator, so the market's "defiance" may be more predictable than problematic in our decision making.

Third, a sudden world crisis throws almost all possible correlations between theoretical direction and reality completely asunder. The tragedy of 9/11 comes to mind, as does the impact of Hurricane Katrina on world energy prices.

In other words, this cycle model is not a standalone predictor of market direction: It only gives us some general guidelines. *We need more inputs into the timing decision model.*

ADDING TECHNICAL ANALYSIS TO THE DECISION-MAKING EQUATION

I use technical analysis, even while always trying to put what the technical "tea leaves" suggest into a fundamental perspective. In the end, I think it is important to put our timing decisions within the context of a probability that is based on both fundamental and technical factors, because the *fundamental context might influence the extremes of our expectation.*

For instance, in the 1990s I frequently wrote in my market comments to institutional subscribers that the global embrace of capitalism and market-driven economies was a major fundamental *macro*development, standing to make the global economic pie just that much bigger because the worldwide levels of business activity would increase. The people of newly developed, newly prospering countries will want to buy products and services as their standards of living increase. And they will be offering goods and services that might appeal to us. So, overall market corrections might be blunted even if the theoretical cycle direction is down. On the other hand, a period of stagnant economic growth and high inflation might see prices exacerbated on the downside, defying theoretical up cycles.

In Figures 8.8 through 8.27 *I have matched my net influence cycle model with actual market prices for the Dow Jones Industrial Average, from 1985 to 2005.* Each figure shows the actual market for the calendar year in the upper graph, with the theoretical cycle model just below (lined up by calendar date).

For 2006 through 2009 (Figures 8.28–8.31), I provide just the theoretical net influence indicator, and some general comments. Along the x-axis on each chart are the theoretical calendar targets for a change in prospective trend direction.

All historical price charts for the Dow Industrials are courtesy of Worden Bros., Inc.'s *Telechart Platinum* technical analysis, data, and charting service. For more information about the Worden service, from the Watauga Equity Management web site's home page (www.wataugamgt.com) click on the hyperlink to *TCNet*, found near the top of the right-hand side of the home page. You could go to the Worden home page directly (www.worden.com), but Worden's marketing folks have advised me that they like to track from where their inquiries originate.

1986

The market's sideways consolidation through most of 1986 matched up fairly well with the theoretical cycle direction. It is important to know that the upper limits of my cycle indicator's value (y-axis), is between 6,000 and 7,000. When it reaches these extreme net values, there seems to be a tendency for overall market strength to persist, even if the theoretical trend indicator is starting to decline.

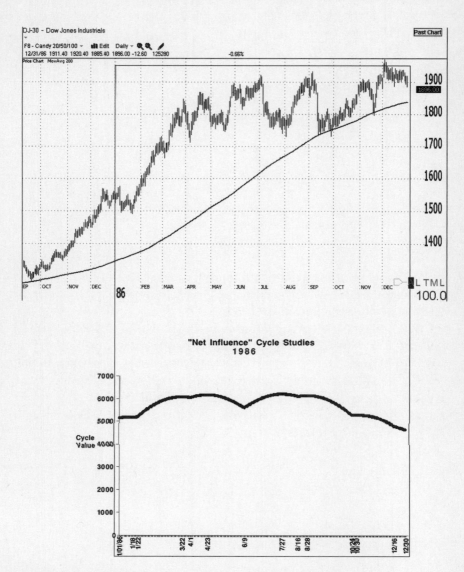

FIGURE 8.8   Market versus Theoretical Cycle Indicator, 1986

Source: Chart courtesy of Worden Brothers, Inc., *Telechart Platinum*. For more information, please go to www.wataugamgt.com and click on the hyperlink to TCNet.

1987

The early phase of market strength during the first half of 1987 was not surprising since we were in "defiance" mode, with the cycle indicator reaching near maximum values in 1986.

But a sagging cycle study in the second half of 1987 persuaded me on October 1, 1987 (DJIA: 2640), to make a daring market call when I received a Primary Sell in my technical analysis—based market timing model. I told all who would listen at The Illinois Company (Chicago) that I expected a disastrous market decline and that the next time to buy stocks with a higher probability of intermediate-term profit was December 8, 1987, give or take a few days.

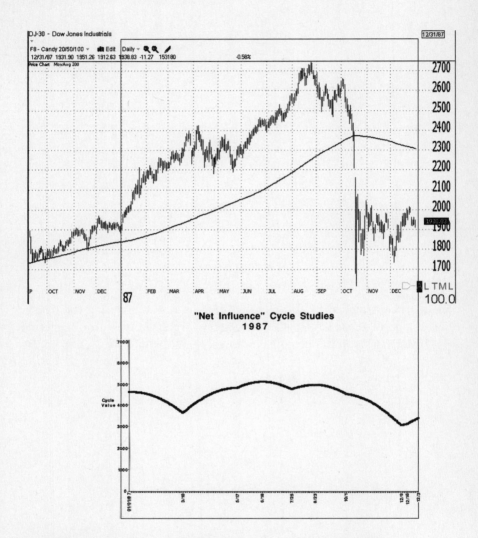

FIGURE 8.9   Market versus Theoretical Cycle Indicator, 1987

Source: Chart courtesy of Worden Brothers, Inc., *Telechart Platinum*. For more information, please go to www.wataugamgt.com and click on the hyperlink to TCNet.

1988

The market struggled to do much in 1988, as it was digesting the Crash. This is one of those times when the downward cycle indicator suggested that if the market didn't actually go down, then it would struggle to go up.

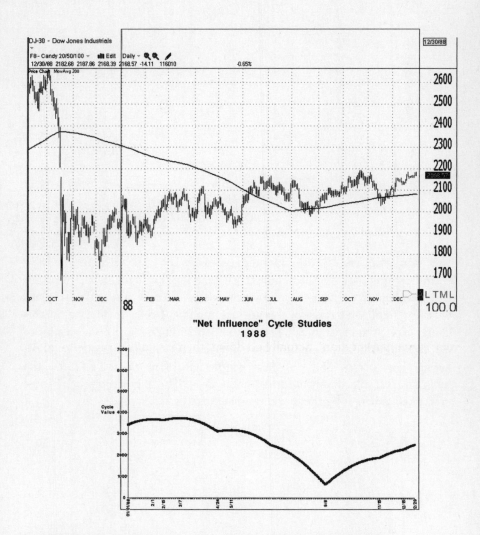

FIGURE 8.10   Market versus Theoretical Cycle Indicator, 1988
Source: Chart courtesy of Worden Brothers, Inc., *Telechart Platinum.* For more information, please go to www.wataugamgt.com and click on the hyperlink to TCNet.

1989

After struggling in 1988, the market's recovery got into full swing in 1989 before running into overhead resistance near the old highs. It is important to remember that previous price levels where a lot of trading took place represent significant resistance points. In a chart, I refer to them as places "congestion area resistance." These are historical price levels where a lot of people bought before watching their investment values plummet with declining share prices. Some of these people will be motivated to sell when the price recovers, thankful to just break even. This increased supply must be worked through by the market, which usually takes time.

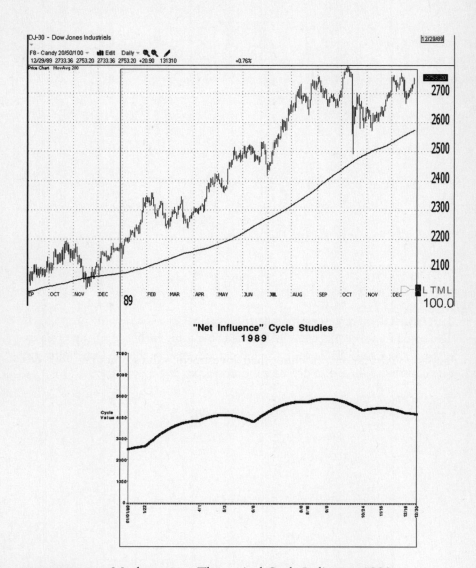

FIGURE 8.11   Market versus Theoretical Cycle Indicator, 1989

Source: Chart courtesy of Worden Brothers, Inc., *Telechart Platinum.* For more information, please go to www.wataugamgt.com and click on the hyperlink to TCNet.

1990

The first half of the year matched theoretical cycle direction pretty well. The top and subsequent harsh decline came a bit earlier than the cycle direction predicted. While the cycle indicator was near the extreme highs, the normal sort of direction defiance did not occur in this instance.

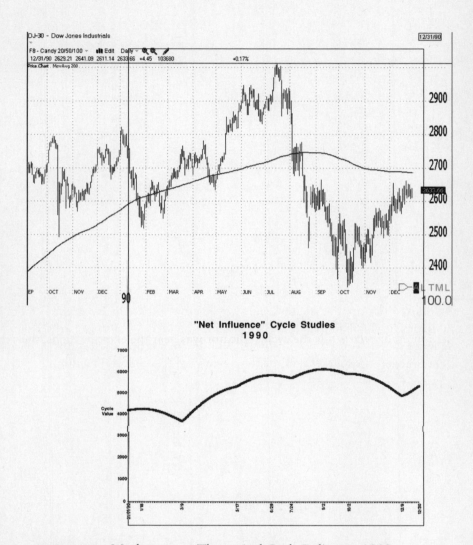

FIGURE 8.12   Market versus Theoretical Cycle Indicator, 1990

Source: Chart courtesy of Worden Brothers, Inc., *Telechart Platinum*. For more information, please go to www.wataugamgt.com and click on the hyperlink to TCNet.

1991

We started out up, but the theoretical cycle direction might have kept a lid on things until late in the year. The cycle bottom turned out to be early. The defiance factor worked out this time: With the theoretical cycle value in its upper ranges, the market ignored the downward theoretical direction.

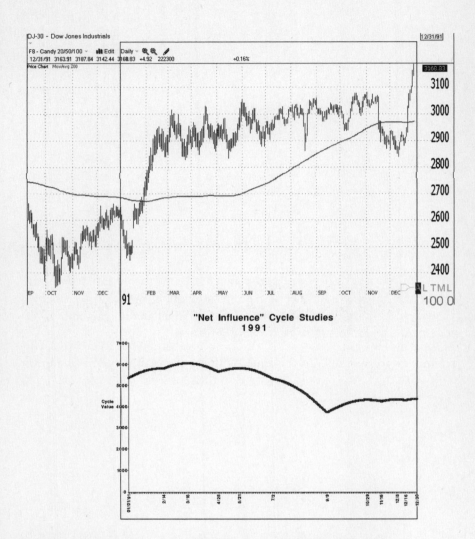

FIGURE 8.13   Market versus Theoretical Cycle Indicator, 1991

Source: Chart courtesy of Worden Brothers, Inc., *Telechart Platinum.* For more information, please go to www.wataugamgt.com and click on the hyperlink to TCNet.

1992

The 1992 market reality was pretty much true to theoretical form, but with better than might have been expected strength in Q4. This is probably because of the previously mentioned defiance factor due to the high cycle index value, regardless of its downward direction.

1993

Upside acceleration didn't really begin here until the theoretical direction

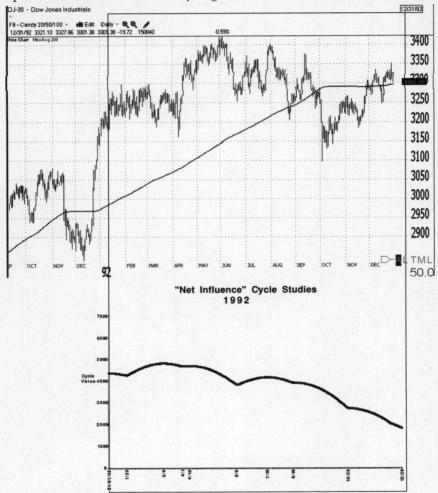

FIGURE 8.14   Market versus Theoretical Cycle Indicator, 1992

Source: Chart courtesy of Worden Brothers, Inc., *Telechart Platinum*. For more information, please go to www.wataugamgt.com and click on the hyperlink to TCNet.

1993

Upside acceleration didn't really begin here until the theoretical direction turned up, although price went against theoretical direction late in the year.

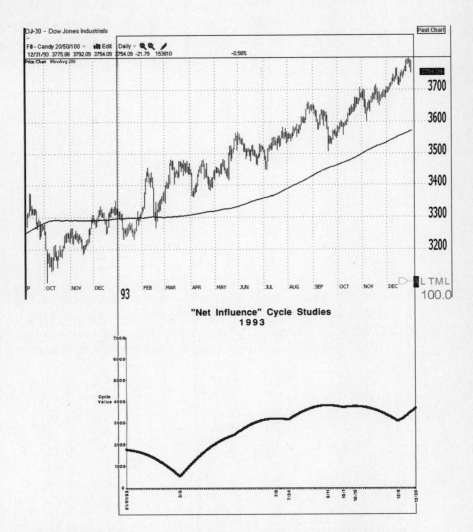

FIGURE 8.15 Market versus Theoretical Cycle Indicator, 1993

Source: Chart courtesy of Worden Brothers, Inc., *Telechart Platinum*. For more information, please go to www.wataugamgt.com and click on the hyperlink to TCNet.

1994

Flat cycle model, flat market for the year, although there were some intervening fluctuations that were not identified by the cycle model alone. Especially in these types of trading range markets, technical analysis timing
systems can help managers add value through hedging and enhancement
techniques.

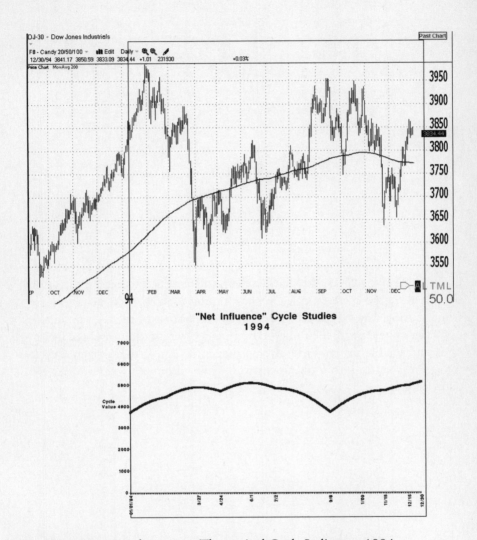

FIGURE 8.16   Market versus Theoretical Cycle Indicator, 1994

Source: Chart courtesy of Worden Brothers, Inc., *Telechart Platinum*. For more information, please go to www.wataugamgt.com and click on the hyperlink to TCNet.

1995

Defiance 101? In 1995, the market clearly defied the theoretical direction suggested by the cycle model. Our best timing tools in these instances are Continuation Buy signals (see next chapter). Because of the high cycle values, even approaching their maximum range, Continuation Buy signals can be fairly reliable in this kind of environment—even if the indicated cycle direction is starting to look downward. This epitomizes what we call the defiance factor.

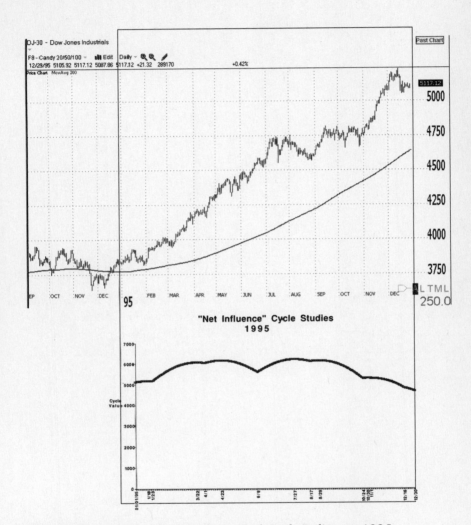

FIGURE 8.17 Market versus Theoretical Cycle Indicator, 1995

Source: Chart courtesy of Worden Brothers, Inc., *Telechart Platinum.* For more information, please go to www.wataugamgt.com and click on the hyperlink to TCNet.

1996

The first half of the year the market's uptrend was blunted, but some good things were going on in the economy, including the global embrace of market-driven, capitalistic systems. Notice the spring the market got when it corrected back (mostly sideways) to its steeply rising 200-day moving average.

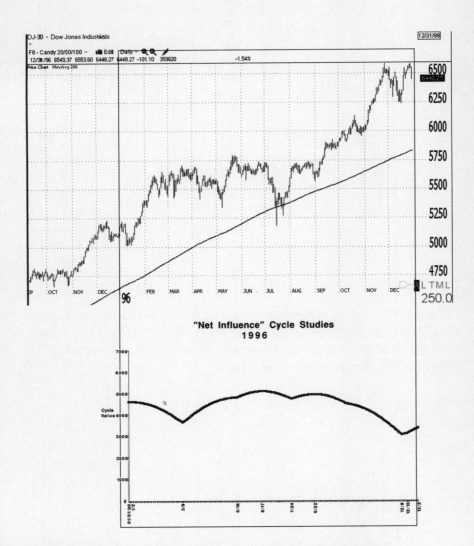

FIGURE 8.18   Market versus Theoretical Cycle Indicator, 1996

Source: Chart courtesy of Worden Brothers, Inc., *Telechart Platinum.* For more information, please go to www.wataugamgt.com and click on the hyperlink to TCNet.

1997

The corrective activity in 1997 came a bit later than expected, based on the cycle model. But we were in a bull market, and Continuation Buy signals were in effect, so this was not surprising. In this instance, the theoretical cycle direction seemed to have little effect.

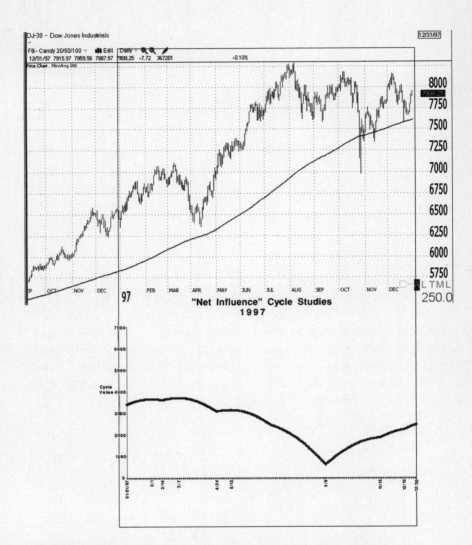

FIGURE 8.19   Market versus Theoretical Cycle Indicator, 1997

Source: Chart courtesy of Worden Brothers, Inc., *Telechart Platinum.* For more information, please go to www.wataugamgt.com and click on the hyperlink to TCNet.

1998

The market was pretty strong in the first half of 1998, although the July-October correction was a bit steeper than one might have anticipated. On the other hand, the October-December rebound was equally vigorous. This is why our technical analysis-based timing models are also important. Visually, the price decline below the 200-day moving average (MA) was about the same as its previous height above the moving average. The fact that the MA was rising fairly steadily was a good clue that the depth of the correction would be relatively modest.

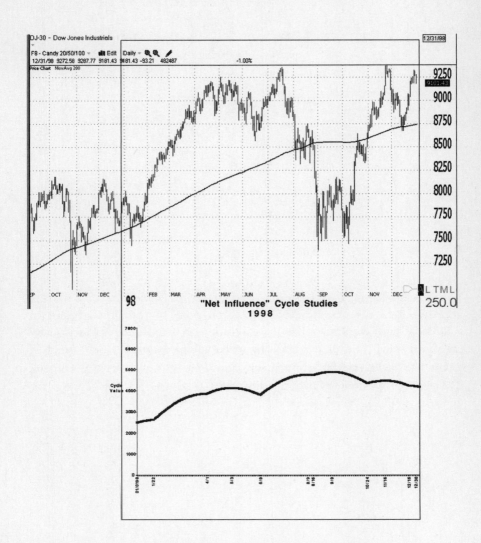

FIGURE 8.20 Market versus Theoretical Cycle Indicator, 1998
Source: Chart courtesy of Worden Brothers, Inc., *Telechart Platinum.* For more
information, please go to www.wataugamgt.com and click on the hyperlink
to TCNet.

1999

The general character of the cycle model was up. Notice how the market accelerated to the upside after the March cycle bottom, then began to round off with the cycle. The price bottom occurred uncharacteristically early, but this is not really surprising when you also consider that the cycle value is pressing its upper limits, suggesting we were in a generally strong market environment.

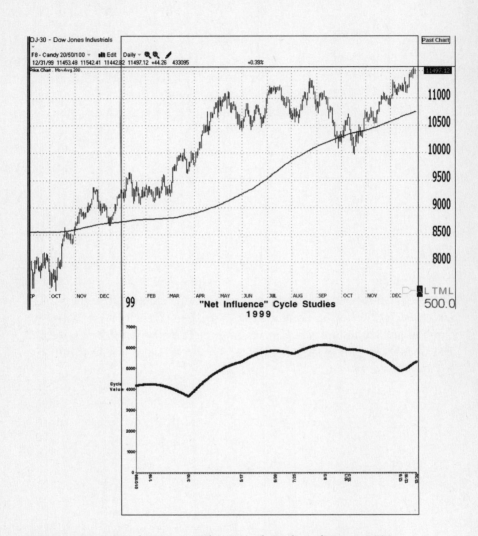

FIGURE 8.21   Market versus Theoretical Cycle Indicator, 1999

Source: Chart courtesy of Worden Brothers, Inc., *Telechart Platinum.* For more information, please go to www.wataugamgt.com and click on the hyperlink to TCNet.

2000

Generally, 2000 was a corrective year, as the cycle model suggests. The September cycle bottom was a little early, but given Reverse Wave Sell signal in our studies in mid-January, and the Primary Sell in our system of overall market timing signals in late March, we were not in a hurry to buy stocks.

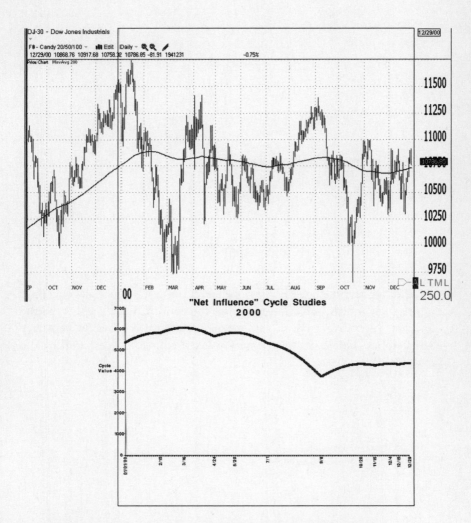

FIGURE 8.22 Market versus Theoretical Cycle Indicator, 2000

Source: Chart courtesy of Worden Brothers, Inc., *Telechart Platinum*. For more information, please go to www.wataugamgt.com and click on the hyperlink to TCNet.

2001

The market pretty much mirrored the general pattern of the theoretical net influence cycle model, direction-wise, but the major calendar targets in the cycle chart were a bit early vs. the intermediate-term bottoms in February and September. The corrective activity was, of course, exacerbated by the events of 9/11.

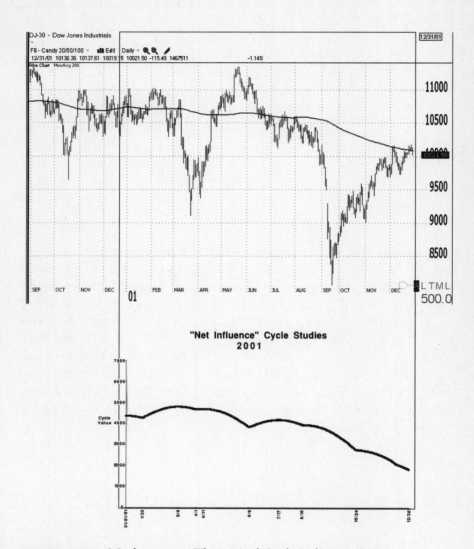

FIGURE 8.23   Market versus Theoretical Cycle Indicator, 2001

Source: Chart courtesy of Worden Brothers, Inc., *Telechart Platinum.* For more information, please go to www.wataugamgt.com and click on the hyperlink to TCNet.

2002

This was one of those times when the market defied theoretical cycle direction, but there may be a correlation with the absolute cycle value around zero, similar to what we observe at market tops. We speculate that the decline would have been a lot worse if the net influence cycle direction had been pointed down. Keep in mind that the world was still feeling the effects of 9/11, and a vicious bear market decline in 2001. We had Reverse Wave and Primary Sell signals in our system of timing signals, so "caution" was our middle name, especially with Continuation Sell signals operative and foreshadowing a selling capitulation phase. The selling capitulation took the market far below the lower boundary of the Reverse Wave megaphone pattern.

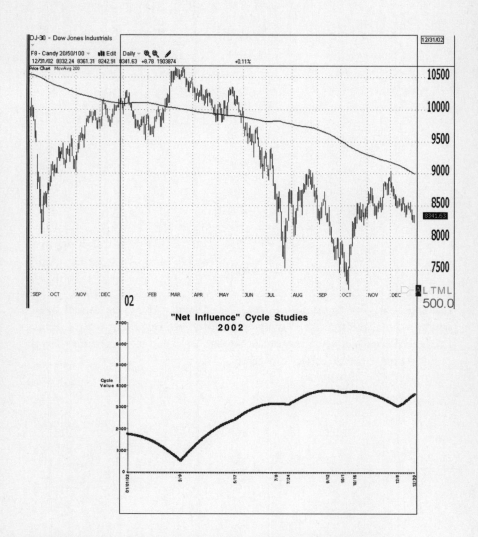

FIGURE 8.24   Market versus Theoretical Cycle Indicator, 2002
Source: Chart courtesy of Worden Brothers, Inc., *Telechart Platinum.* For more
information, please go to www.wataugamgt.com and click on the hyperlink
to TCNet.

2003

The most striking thing about 2003 is that when the cycle model turned down in June, the market's advance was blunted, turning mostly sideways until the theoretical cycle bottom in September. Then it reaccelerated to the upside as the cycle direction turned up.

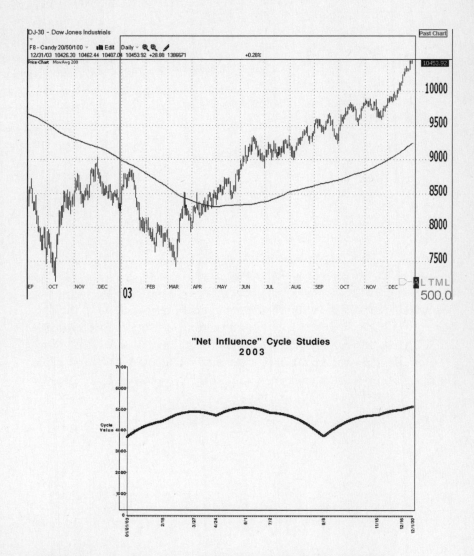

FIGURE 8.25   Market versus Theoretical Cycle Indicator, 2003

Source: Chart courtesy of Worden Brothers, Inc., *Telechart Platinum.* For more information, please go to www.wataugamgt.com and click on the hyperlink to TCNet.

2004

The market tracked the 2004 theoretical model pretty well, until the fierce year-end rally. As it turned out, it was setting up for a more corrective 2005. Notice where the cycle values are in the overall scheme of things, pressing up against their maximum potential. This offered a good probability that an up market might defy the downward-pushing cycle direction.

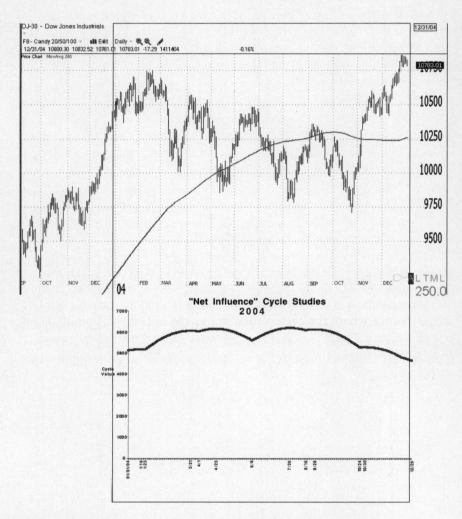

FIGURE 8.26   Market versus Theoretical Cycle Indicator, 2004
Source: Chart courtesy of Worden Brothers, Inc., *Telechart Platinum*. For more information, please go to www.wataugamgt.com and click on the hyperlink to TCNet.

2005

The market's price action generally reflected the corrective suggestion of the theoretical cycle model in 2005, sideways. The price bottom in April was a little bit late, which it should be. While the significant price bottom in October matched the minicycle bottom on October 1, it was largely off to the races until year-end, ignoring the December cycle bottom. Most of the year-end rally had been put in by the time of the cycle calendar target on December 8.

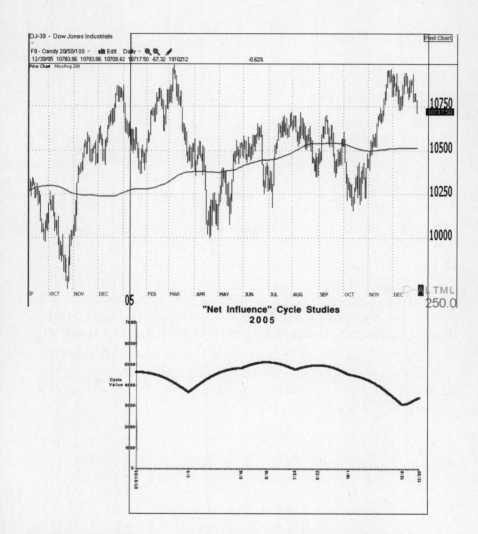

FIGURE 8.27   Market versus Theoretical Cycle Indicator, 2005

Source: Chart courtesy of Worden Brothers, Inc., *Telechart Platinum.* For more information, please go to www.wataugamgt.com and click on the hyperlink to TCNet.

2006

Our cycle study suggests that 2006 will have some adverse influences, especially after April. This fits with our fundamental perspective as this is being written—an inverted yield curve and still upward pressure on our "big 4" economic measures: the Price of Money (interest rates), the Price of Energy (oil), the Price of Food and the Price of Labor (wage inflation). By the time this book is published, most of 2006 will have passed into history. Our favored scenario is for strength in the first couple of months, then a challenging, adverse period into the summer/fall, with perhaps a vigorous rally into year-end. Did it happen?

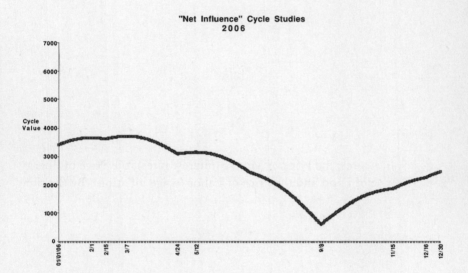

FIGURE 8.28   Theoretical Cycle Indicator, 2006

2007

We often see a vigorous market in the year prior to a presidential election, and our cycle model suggests that 2007 will have upward influences, too.

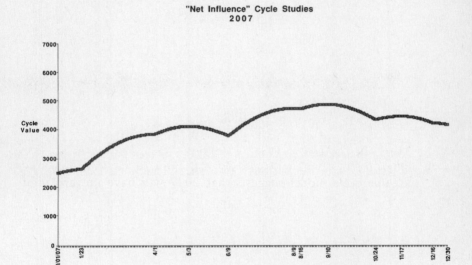

FIGURE 8.29   Theoretical Cycle Indicator, 2007

2008

As befitting a presidential election year, 2008 looks to be largely up, with a post-election corrective period come fall. A major calendar target is March 9.

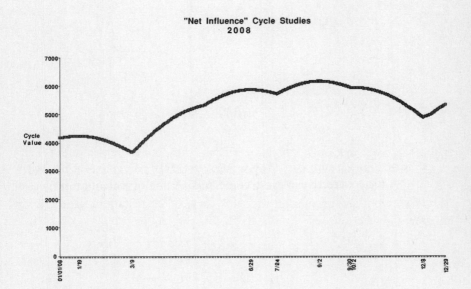

FIGURE 8.30 Theoretical Cycle Indicator, 2008

2009

The cycle direction looks largely down for 2009, but there is a high potential that the market will defy gravity because the cycle value (y-axis) starts off in the upper third of the range for this model. So we would not be surprised to see a strong market in 2009—even if it is the first year after a presidential election.

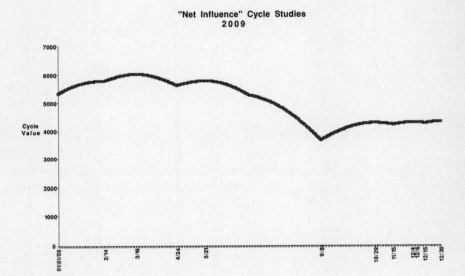

FIGURE 8.31   Theoretical Cycle Indicator, 2009

9

Technical Timing Signals

I joined Dean Witter as a retail stockbroker in 1977, in Bakersfield, California. By late 1978, I had relocated to La Jolla, California. During Dean Witter's broker training, when I was still based in Bakersfield, I was exposed to both fundamental and technical analysis, but it was only after I moved to La Jolla that my real stock market education began.

In recent years, as the retail brokerage business evolved toward fee-based compensation versus assets under management, retail brokers have transitioned to more of an "advisor" or "consultant" role. But in 1978, a broker's primary compensation was still derived from commissionable transactions, most frequently from purchases and sales of stocks and bonds, although increasingly from selling mutual funds and insurance products. Some brokers were making a small fortune by peddling "tax-advantaged investments" such as real estate or oil and gas limited partnerships, but I had already become fascinated by the significant capital appreciation potential of publicly traded stocks.

I have to explain that when I first started in the brokerage business—like a lot of the new brokers in those days—I did not have much in the way of formal business or finance education. I was an English major in high school and a History major in college. I was told that being a broker was a sales profession, and that I would learn everything I needed to know about the stock market and the investment products I would be selling in the firm's training program.

As an aside, I applaud the brokerage industry's migration to asset- and fee-based revenue models (even if it was coerced into it by the commoditization of trade execution and the disappearance of traditional commissions). While I probably would not even have qualified for today's training programs without significantly greater business education than I had in those days, I nonetheless endorse the industry's pushing brokers away from the trading-based commission models of Grandpa's day to the modern advisory and consultant roles. While I wish they would do more than push mediocrity onto the investment public (and that they would teach their investment executives more about what makes a market go up and down), there are significantly fewer risks to the brokerage customer with the newer business models.

Back in the late 1970s, as a rookie broker I assumed that the vast majority of the analysts getting paid the big bucks for producing research reports back in New York were a lot smarter than me. But time after time their work disappointed, and it didn't seem to matter what brokerage firm's research I was using. With their supposedly well-researched ideas, my position-building customers had to watch the value of their stocks go down 30 to 80% before they saw any share appreciation at all, if any.

These analysts back in New York are getting paid *how much* to produce this stuff? I asked. More and more, this buy-and-hold concept we were taught during broker training seemed to be more of a bailout for a firm's analysts, who didn't seem to have a clue about what makes stock valuations fluctuate. They don't have any sense whatsoever, I decided, about *timing* purchase and sale transactions for the individual stocks they were recommending. Buy and hold and eventually you will earn a positive return from these good companies.

Of course, that was the proverbial $64,000 question: Were they *really* good companies? It wasn't supposed to be, but the lines were already starting to be blurred between research and the corporate finance mission of the brokerage. The conflicts of interest reached critical mass only when laid bare by the declining prices of the bear market beginning in 2000—and investors began to ask questions. Tyco, WorldCom, Enron . . . it seemed a never-ending list of corporate scandal, and it dragged many a research analyst into the muck, exposed for the conflicts of interest.

So my interest in stock market research really began out of the frustra-

tion and disappointment I experienced in trying to sell the brokerage firms' research ideas. To say they were rarely good ideas would be an understatement. Ironically, I started my investment career during the last few years of a secular bear market (1978), when the overall market was pressing down on the valuations of the whole economy and the companies operating within it. *The research pro's analysis might have been good for corporate finance purposes, but their research was of little value to the investor making decisions in the aftermarket,* especially in a bear market.

I had been a pretty good student in high school and college, and considered myself a quick study. I lacked formal corporate finance training, or even a business statistics course, but I figured that anyone with half a brain and some willingness to learn couldn't do any worse than the Wall Street guys who were pushing out nearly worthless reams of paper in those days.

My interests gravitated equally toward fundamental and technical analysis. Companies had to have revenue, earnings, and a value proposition, I reasoned, but I figured that technical analysis held the best potential for improving the timing of client investments in individual stocks, as well as in the overall stock market. Why? Because the data on which most of technical analysis is based is reported daily. It would not be until years later that I would expand on my skill-set for picking small cap stocks, emphasizing the timing and valuation potential of the investment from fundamental studies, as well as from a technical analysis perspective.

Richard "Dick" Vance was a fellow stockbroker, a colleague of mine in the La Jolla office of Loeb Rhoades Hornblower in the late 1970s. He was kind enough to answer my many pestering questions, and gave me an early introduction to the importance of overall market direction to portfolio management. He was particularly focused on market "breadth" studies, especially the McClellan Oscillator and the McClellan Summation Index.

Market breadth studies are statistical calculations based on the difference between the number of advancing issues versus the number of declining issues on an exchange, such as the NYSE or NASDAQ. There are all sorts of ways to slice and dice the basic calculation, with different indicators derived from this simple subtraction or the calculation's component parts, as well as from volume-related studies derived from breadth.

But my first exposure was through Mr. Vance and to the McClellan studies. By hand, Dick updated graphs for these and other indicators every day on the hallway wall outside our private offices. He also taught me how to calculate them. The late Kennedy Gammage, the La Jolla-based editor and publisher of the *Richland Report*, and a recognized scholar of the Mc-Clellan breadth studies, occasionally visited Mr. Vance. I would eavesdrop as frequently as I could on their conversations about the technical health of the stock market, without being too obvious.

In 1979, I met Richard Russell, editor and publisher of *Dow Theory Letters*, over breakfast one morning in a hole-in-the-wall coffee shop on La Jolla's Wall Street. I had heard of a La Jolla-based market newsletter writer named Richard Russell. This man claimed *not* to be *that* Richard Russell, but I saw a picture of the famous Dow Theory guru years later and realized that he and the fellow that I had met were one and the same. I can only imagine the chuckles he got from listening to a neophyte, still-learning, market timing wannabe.

More and more, I found myself attracted to technical analysis subjects. I read newsletters published by Gammage and Russell, of course, as well as Stan Weinstein's *Professional Tape Reader*. I gained bits and pieces of market knowledge from all of them, but for my mindset and investment objectives there was something missing.

Then, in 1982, I became exposed to two very different philosophies that would alter, and sharpen, the course of my learning about the stock market. First, a client of mine in Chicago introduced me to Richard Ney's theory that the stock market is a big con game, manipulated by the New York Stock Exchange specialists. I thoroughly discounted that notion, believing that the global market and macroeconomic forces are so much bigger than a handful of individuals on the Exchange floor. Maybe in shorter-term time frames there was merit to Ney's manipulation and conspiracy theories, but not for the longer-term, I reasoned. *And yet, there were elements of Ney's philosophy that made perfect sense to me.*

It was as a result of studying Ney that I finally latched onto contrarian thinking as a philosophy most suited for me. His core thesis that the specialists accumulate stock in large quantities at market bottoms (before allowing prices to go higher on relatively light volume) is now at the foundation of my own "Smart Money" contrarian thought. I just expanded his thesis to include a broader, more logical portion of the investment population (even if the thrill of his conspiracy theory sold more newsletters for Mr. Ney!).

To my thinking, Smart Money includes specialists, but it also includes a whole host of other market participants, such as insiders, high-net-worth individuals trading for their own accounts, and a vast multitude of very bright professional money managers, among others. All of these men and women are out there, looking for lower-valued investment opportunities.

Like others of my ilk, I use technical analysis to identify the "smart money patterns of accumulation and distribution." These patterns anticipate probable changes in trend direction, up or down. *Certain market patterns repeat themselves.* Understanding these patterns, and the probability that one or more may apply to a then-current market environment, is *key to putting the 90% solution—overall market direction—to work to the benefit of your portfolio.*

MARKET REALITIES

Just after the Crash of 1929, an excited *Wall Street Journal* reporter is said to have accosted Mr. J.P. Morgan himself on Wall Street. "Mr. Morgan! Mr. Morgan!" the reporter cried. "What will the market do today?" In reply, Morgan snarled, "Fluctuate!"

Over any time frame, prices change. They go up and they go down, even if sometimes more sideways than decisively trending. It is all part of the same game we call *the market.*

Fear and Greed are the market's primary drivers. Fear crushes prices to despairingly low valuations, and then Greed propels prices to unsustainable optimism. These psycho-emotional forces are powerful, to be sure, preying on investors' collective alternating uncertainty and optimism. In large measure, and in graphic terms, the stock market is nothing more than *a series of overreactions of investor sentiment* above and below some unseen, "real value" line.

What is real value? Is it some number that adds together all of the Dow Industrials' component companies' shareholder equity? Is it a calculation of aggregate tangible book value? Whatever you use to represent the real value of the companies in the Dow Industrials or the S&P 500, or any other popular market index, I dare say that *this real value changes very little from day to day.* In fact, if you were to plot the number on a daily basis, you would probably have a remarkably straight line that trends slightly up or slightly down depending on the secular expansions and contractions in the business cycle.

So what is it, then, about this thing we call the "stock market"? Why are there these *seemingly sudden and wild plunges in valuation, or the alternate climbs to lofty prices?* It is all about those emotional animals we call Fear and Greed, and the series of overreactions of investor sentiment above and below the unseen, *real value.*

As indicated before, Smart Money accumulates value at low prices and distributes value at high prices, collectively, whether specialists, institutions, insiders, or high-net-worth individuals. Smart Money could even include Ma and Pa America and a host of foreign investors.

But the timing challenge is to identify the technical patterns that represent those accumulation and distribution moments in time. For me, the most interesting technical constructs to help investors potentially take advantage of the market's natural volatility are trading "envelopes." This is a concept to which I was first introduced in 1982, by Dr. William Schmidt. He called them "bends," and applied them to both his Peerless timing system for the overall market, as well as to his Tiger software that looks at technical patterns in individual stocks.

Most good technical analysis graphic packages today facilitate trading envelopes now, in one form or another. Essentially, they give the trader or investor boundaries for normal price movement, and they can be constructed over just about any time frame. Whether you are looking at hourly, daily, weekly, monthly, quarterly, or even five-minute bar charts, you *begin with calculating a moving average, and then plotting equidistant lines, percentage-wise, above and below the moving average.* A similar chart can be created by plotting *x* number of standard deviations above and below a moving average. (See Figure 9.1.)

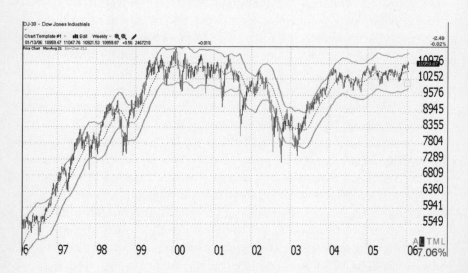

FIGURE 9.1   Market Volatility and Trading Envelopes, DJIA Weekly Chart
Source: Chart courtesy of TCNet, a product of Worden Brothers, Inc. For more information, go to www.wataugamgt.com and click on the hyperlink to TCNet.

The more volatile the market or stock you are graphing, the greater the number of standard deviations or higher percentage bands you will need to calculate, to contain the historical price action. Some graphics packages give you more flexibility than others. I primarily use Worden Brothers, Inc.'s *Telechart Platinum*, which is one of the most powerful, easy-to-use, and value-priced products available. Worden has an unparalleled commitment to product quality and customer support. I have been a user since 1990, growing with them through several upgrades since it was an MS-DOS–based system. Every new version has important enhancements, new utilities, better design, greater flexibility, and more power.

There will be more commentary on Worden-facilitated technical tools in later chapters, but for now let's get back to market volatility and trading envelopes. You generally want to construct them so that they contain at least 90%, and preferably more than 95% of all trading activity over, say, 300 days or 300 weeks (or 300 5-minute periods!). You have to have a large enough sampling of historical data to construct something meaningful. In a "trading range" type of market environment, you may look to establish long positions (buy) near the lower band and sell or hedge them when the overall market prices (we'll use the Dow Jones Industrial Average here) tag the upper band.

An important note on volatility and trading envelopes: Volatility changes. As it increases, you have to adjust your trading envelopes wider. As volatility decreases, the envelopes must tighten. They also are likely to change with increasing market liquidity and market efficiencies. When I first started using envelopes (what I now call my Dynamic Trading Channel) in 1982, the ideal band width was near 4% above and 4% below the calculated moving average. Today, the marketplace has become more efficient with significantly greater liquidity. Therefore, the volatility bands have contracted somewhat, to a little over 3.5%.

Now in a trading range market, envelopes are particularly useful because they offer a suggestion as to the extremes of volatility; but what happens if they are exceeded, if the market prices go *through* the envelope? A strong market may crawl up the upper band, pulling the band ever higher to the market's full valuation, or plunge below the lower band in a selling capitulation phase (dragging the lower band with it).

My timing system for the overall market recognizes the potential for these strong trending markets to occur, so I have specific rules that create Continuation Buy or Continuation Sell signals. *I have even developed certain cyclical and technical conditions that increase or decrease the probability that the upper and lower bands will fail to contain prices.* These are

times when price going to an envelope limit is not necessarily going to result in an immediate trend reversal.

   In effect, by using trading channels, or envelopes, I identify *potential*
extremes of investor sentiment. These historical extremes become potential
points at which we can make contrarian decisions that anticipate changes
in trend direction. *But reaching a historical extreme in price is not the sole
decision trigger for my system of timing signals.*

   I regard the price fluctuations as the *external* market. This is the price
behavior that you, me, and everyone else can readily see. In Figure 9.2, the
Dow Industrials broke out of a springtime trading range (circled area,
Point A) to advance vigorously throughout the summer of 1987. After a
pullback into mid-September, the market was tagging the upper band when
it closed at 2,640 on October 1 (Point B). With its seeming vigor renewed,
the price of the Dow Industrials alone showed no indication that the bull
market was over. Would this prove an important turning point, or would
the market continue to advance, carrying the upper band with it like it had
in the early part of the year and in the summer?

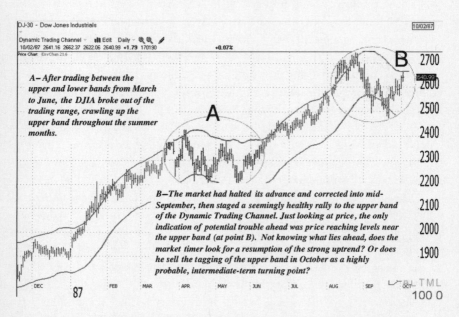

FIGURE 9.2   Decision Point at the Upper Band: Sell, Hold, or Buy?
Source: Chart courtesy of TCNet, a product of Worden Brothers, Inc. For more
information, go to www.wataugamgt.com, and click on the hyperlink to TCNet.
Graphic enhancements made by the author.

In order to make high-probability anticipatory decisions, *I also look at what I call the "internal" market*. This includes *technical studies based on breadth (advances vs. declines), volume, momentum, rate of change, volatility, and other measures*. Different students of the market look at different indicators to determine whether a trend reversal from a price extreme (i.e., when the market rises to the upper band) is probable.

My mentor and good friend in this concept was Dr. William Schmidt (Tiger Software and Peerless Market Timing Systems). I will discuss Dr. Schmidt's work later, but he expanded on the work of other students of the market, such as Joe Granville, as well as contributing some very original thinking of his own. Some students of the market have constructed breadth-related tools, while others integrate volume-related or momentum disciplines. Still others have toyed with statistical constructs derived from price-only calculations. All of them are designed to give hints as to current market psychology and the probability of future trend direction.

In Figure 9.3, we see that the October 1, 1987, tagging of the upper

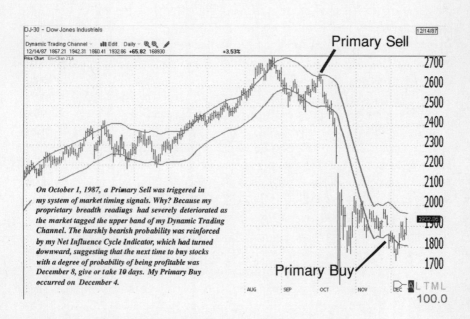

FIGURE 9.3 The Upper Band as Turning Point, 1987

Source: Chart courtesy of TCNet, a product of Worden Brothers, Inc. For more information, go to www.wataugamgt.com, and click on the hyperlink to TCNet. Graphic enhancements made by the author.

band of our channel (trading envelope) was indeed a turning point. My market timing system triggered a Primary Sell on October 1, which at the time was my most bearish signal. It is an expansion of a concept I first learned from Dr. Schmidt. Alone, it didn't say that there was *going* to be a market crash, with the proverbial "blood running in the Street" (which tragically manifested itself when a disgruntled investor gunned down the manager of a Merrill Lynch office in south Florida).

The sell signal *suggests only that there is a high probability that the market is transitioning into a corrective phase, which could be harsh*. We always have to keep in mind that markets also correct through price consolidation over time, or with some combination of consolidation and price decline.

In the case of 1987, I was aggressive in my bearish outlook on October 1 because the Primary Sell occurred while my theoretical, Net Influence Cycle Indicator was pointing downward (refer back the net influence cycle study for 1987 in Chapter 8, Figure 8.9). It was not due to bottom until December 8, give or take 10 days, a full two months away.

When I talk about market timing with traditional money managers, brokers, or investors, I frequently hear something to the effect that "No one can time the market consistently." Frankly, those comments are made by people who have absolutely no idea what they are talking about. *Highly profitable timing decisions can be made.* And, over time, the investor can *accumulate considerable added value over buy and hold methodologies*.

From an academic perspective, the only-fundamental-analysis-for-me naysayers should not be too quick to judge. A company's shares could be trading at a historically low multiple of price to trailing 12 months' earnings or enterprise value to EBITDA, but there is still no guarantee that the share price has reached bottom, much less that it will appreciate in value. The investor or analyst making a decision to buy based on that information is doing the same thing as the technical analysis student of the market: *establishing probability of future price direction based on observations of historically derived patterns or market conditions*. He's just using a different tool.

Always remember, the mission for using any kind of research approach is not to predict the market direction, but to *establish a degree of probability* that the market will trend in one direction or another, whether using technical, fundamental, quantitative, astrological, cyclical, or any other kind of analysis. *There is a subtle, but important difference between the arrogance of predicting market direction versus humbly establishing its probable future price trend*.

Since about 1983, I have managed mutual fund timing or allocation accounts for family and friends, off and on. I did this for a few brokerage customers, too, over the years. Then, in 2002, Cliff Montgomery of Theta Research (Philadelphia), a performance analytics firm specializing in mutual fund asset allocation models, called to ask me if his firm could monitor my accounts held at Rydex. I said sure, but explained that my Rydex accounts represented only a small amount of family money and that this was not my core business. He said, "That's okay; we just want to expand the universe of asset allocation firms and timing models that we follow, to make our service more robust and with greater perspective."

Well, I have not been right about the market all of the time since then but, over time, I think I have demonstrated that timing can add value. In Figure 9.4, a performance chart of my less aggressive service, *Index Plus*, versus the Standard & Poor's 500 (the index being timed), you can see that over the two-year period from February 17, 2004, to February 16, 2006, we earned a good amount of extra return relative to the S&P 500, after all management fees. When looking at these charts, it is important to know that we primarily use Rydex Dynamic Dow-30 Fund in this service, a leveraged fund structured to perform at a 2× beta versus the S&P 500. However, in Index Plus, we only make 75% capital contributions to most signals, so it performs like a 1.5× beta versus the S&P. Our accounts are only modestly leveraged, but they go up in value faster than the market when we are right, and down faster when we stay invested in market downturns.

At times over the two-year period we were actually even further ahead of the market averages. But *in spite of timing miscues in the summer of*

FIGURE 9.4 *Index Plus* Performance versus S&P 500, 24 Months
Source: Copyright © 2006 Theta Investment Research, LLC.

2004 and in the spring of 2005, we are still a good measure ahead (about 8 percentage points of added value) *of the overall market average*, represented by the S&P 500.

Our more aggressive service, Active Index, did even better. Over the same 24-month period, it has added a little more than *20 percentage points more* than an unleveraged index fund would have gained, untimed. Figure 9.5 documents this after-fee performance. But over a 36-month period ending May 30, 2006 (Figure 9.6), *Active Index has added approximately 40 percentage points in extra return* to what a buy-and-hold S&P 500-benchmarked index fund returned.

Keep in mind that Theta Research assumes that all managers in its monitored universe charge a 2.50% annual management fee, calculated and paid quarterly, in order to keep all of the managers and allocation models on an even playing field regarding the efficacy of their timing signals. For management firms that, in reality, have a different compensation structure, their performance may be somewhat understated or overstated by Theta Research analytics.

Watauga Equity Management (my investment advisory firm) charges a 2.50% fee, but we only charge a fee if the account is profitable for the quarter *and* since inception. Moreover, if the amount of any positive quarterly return to the investment client is not at least 2× the 0.625 normal fee for the quarter (the quarterly portion of a 2.50% annual fee), then we discount our fee so that the client *at least makes as much money on their money as we do.*

Growth of Dollar 02/17/2004 to 02/16/2006

Red Line Is Active Index—Black Line Is S&P 500 Index
<<Chart Scale Is Arithmetic>>

FIGURE 9.5 *Active Index* Performance versus S&P 500, 24 Months
Source: Copyright © 2006 Theta Investment Research, LLC.

Growth of Dollar 05/30/2003 to 05/30/2006

Red Line Is Active Index—Black Line Is S&P 500 Index
<<Chart Scale Is Arithmetic>>

FIGURE 9.6 *Active Index* Performance versus S&P 500, 36 Months
Source: Copyright © 2006 Theta Investment Research, LLC.

How are these increased returns possible? And how can I construct a management compensation schedule that might result in the firm not getting paid anything at all in a quarter? The answer to the second question is also the answer to the first. *It is all about confidence in your decision-making tools.* If we earn generously positive returns for our customers, then we deserve to be paid handsomely (and a 2.50% annual rate is well above the average fees charged by the traditional long-only managers unless you also calculate their active expense ratio according to Ross Miller, outlined in the Prologue to Act II). If we don't earn generous returns, then our compensation should be muted, just like the results.

To achieve above-average returns using market timing, *I have developed a system of market timing signals.* It is a model designed to take advantage of what are perceived to be highly probable, intermediate-term trends in the overall market.

In the pages that follow, I share a few examples of my timing signals, with some limited discussion on each. They are randomly selected, and neither the best nor worst of each type.

I have six major types of signal (Figures 9.7–9.21):

1. *Primary Buy* (buy aggressively long, look for the longer-term trend to reverse upward).
2. *Primary Sell* (sell, and sell aggressively short, look for the longer-term trend to reverse downward).

3. *Major Buy* (cover all hedges and short positions, expect a significant intermediate-term advance, probably to new recent highs or at least to the upper band of my *Dynamic Trading Channel*).

4. *Major Sell* (aggressively hedge, selective short selling, expect at least a decline to the lower band of our *Dynamic Trading Channel*, possibly lower).

5. *Continuation Sell* (increase short exposure, a steepening decline is probable, probably even including a selling capitulation phase).

6. *Continuation Buy* (remove all hedges, power advance should be sustained).

These six signals are the core decision makers.

PRIMARY BUY

I have a specific set of rules that generate a Primary Buy signal. They do not occur very often. Usually, *a Primary Buy is triggered after a long, intermediate-term price correction that has ended with a selling capitulation, or*

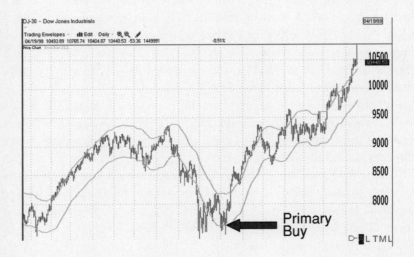

FIGURE 9.7   Primary Buy Signal
Source: Chart courtesy of TCNet, a product of Worden Brothers, Inc. For more information, go to www.wataugamgt.com, and click on the hyperlink to TCNet. Graphic enhancements made by the author.

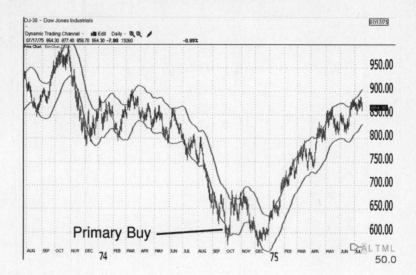

FIGURE 9.8   Primary Buy in 1974

Source: Chart courtesy of TCNet, a product of Worden Brothers, Inc. For more information, go to www.wataugamgt.com, and click on the hyperlink to TCNet. Graphic enhancements made by the author.

climax. It is one of the greatest *contrarian* signals I have ever seen, and it is one that I devised from a very simple observation and quite a bit of conceptual analysis to understand *why* it works.

Don't look here for the specific set of circumstances that trigger the Primary Buy signal, *it is much too valuable to have everyone own it,* because then it would lose its money management value (the markets are big, but ultimately are efficient). Just understand that the *external* (price) market pattern, when integrated with a specific set of *internal* (breadth, volume, momentum, volatility) market conditions, repeats itself time after time.

When *a Primary Buy signal is operative,* I recommend aggressively committing capital to well-diversified stock portfolios and equity mutual funds. This is the epitome of a highly probable, contrarian or *anticipatory* decision. While I have used this signal since 1992, I have *back-tested it more than 100 years.* Only once did it fail to result in a near-immediate, significant intermediate-term advance. In that lone exception, it took about six months of sideways consolidation (base-building) before the advance began. There was very little adverse movement (lower prices) to work against investors' unhedged long positions.

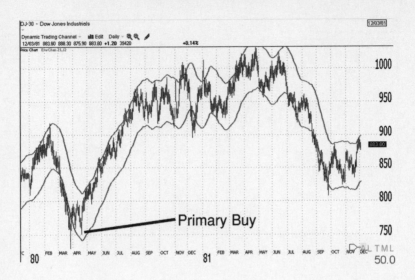

FIGURE 9.9   Primary Buy in 1980

Source: Chart courtesy of TCNet, a product of Worden Brothers, Inc. For more information, go to www.wataugamgt.com, and click on the hyperlink to TCNet. Graphic enhancements made by the author.

PRIMARY SELL

One of the best market calls of my career was on October 1, 1987. I was working at the Chicago headquarters office of The Illinois Company, a regional brokerage firm that has since been acquired and absorbed by other firms. My net influence cycle model suggested corrective forces were at work in the stock market. When a Primary Sell signal was triggered on the first of three consecutive days the Dow Industrials closed at 2,640, I walked around the office telling anybody who would listen that a major market meltdown was (probably) about to take place. I even told the chief operating officer (who is now the chairman of a publicly traded, large brokerage firm based in the Midwest), "The next time to safely buy stocks is December 8, give or take 10 days."

People looked at me incredulously, because the market had been in a major advancing phase. I remember other, more prominent analysts taking credit for "calling the Crash"—but in most of those cases their "calls" were nearly *two weeks later when it was nearly impossible to sell anything.*

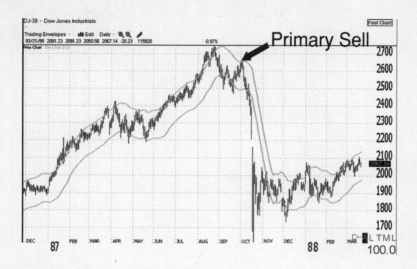

FIGURE 9.10 Primary Sell in 1987

Source: Chart courtesy of TCNet, a product of Worden Brothers, Inc. For more information, go to www.wataugamgt.com, and click on the hyperlink to TCNet. Graphic enhancements made by the author.

If you could, it was at much lower prices. Some trading systems shut down. Orders could not be executed. Ridiculously out-of-whack buy and sell fills were given. So many of those who *said* they called the Crash of '87 really called it at the bottom, for all intents and purposes.

The only analyst I know who did as good a job with the '87 Crash (calling it at the recovery high on October 1, at 2,640 in the Dow), was my friend Dr. William Schmidt, owner of Tiger Software. My Primary Sell is partly a proprietary variation of his Sell S9 signal. My Primary Sell is one of the two most bearish signals in my arsenal and his Sell S9 is still among his most bearish signals. *On a Primary Sell, as with Dr. Schmidt's Sell S9, there is a very high probability that the market will decline at least to the lower band of my Dynamic Trading Channel, and often much lower.*

The *Primary Sell in 1990* led to a classic selling capitulation. I made the call while employed with another regional brokerage firm in Chicago, and followed up with the *Primary Buy that subsequently came after the selling capitulation pattern.*

A Primary Sell does not always have to result in the severest form of selling capitulation. If it is triggered soon after a lengthy and severe selling

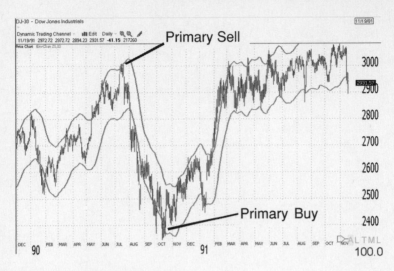

FIGURE 9.11   Primary Sell in 1990

Source: Chart courtesy of TCNet, a product of Worden Brothers, Inc. For more information, go to www.wataugamgt.com, and click on the hyperlink to TCNet. Graphic enhancements made by the author.

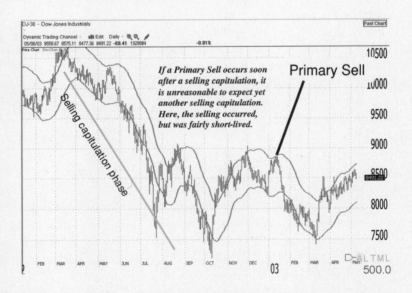

FIGURE 9.12   Primary Sell in 2003 after Selling Capitulation

Source: Chart courtesy of TCNet, a product of Worden Brothers, Inc. For more information, go to www.wataugamgt.com, and click on the hyperlink to TCNet. Graphic enhancements made by the author.

capitulation phase has already occurred, then my expectations for the signal are fairly muted. In 2003, our methodology triggered a Primary Sell in January. Because it occurred so soon after a harsh selling capitulation phase in 2002, a more severe decline was unlikely, so we were recommending aggressive accumulation of good-quality stocks during this pullback into March 2003.

MAJOR BUY

My Major Buy signal generally *reinforces a Primary Buy* after a significantly harsh selling capitulation. Most often it occurs three to eight weeks after the Primary Buy, and is also a very reliable anticipatory signal. Remove all hedges; commit to aggressive long positions. Upside fireworks are probable.

A Major Buy in my system of timing signals often reinforces a Primary Buy. An immediately strong advance frequently occurs, and often leads to a Continuation Buy.

FIGURE 9.13 Major Buy Signal
Source: Chart courtesy of TCNet, a product of Worden Brothers, Inc. For more information, go to www.wataugamgt.com, and click on the hyperlink to TCNet. Graphic enhancements made by the author.

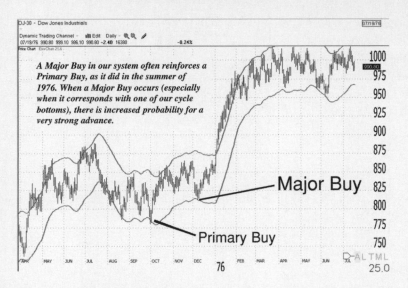

A Major Buy in our system often reinforces a Primary Buy, as it did in the summer of 1976. When a Major Buy occurs (especially when it corresponds with one of our cycle bottoms), there is increased probability for a very strong advance.

FIGURE 9.14   Major Buy in 1975–1976
Source: Chart courtesy of TCNet, a product of Worden Brothers, Inc. For more information, go to www.wataugamgt.com, and click on the hyperlink to TCNet. Graphic enhancements made by the author.

MAJOR SELL—REVERSE WAVE

A couple of years ago, I was frustrated by the market selling off significantly without triggering a major sell signal in my system of timing signals. Obviously, I was missing a weapon in my arsenal of technical tools. So when I learned the power of Reverse Wave signals from my good friend and colleague, Roger Reynolds, some lights went on. It is set up by a five-point "broadening top," or "megaphone" formation. Points 1, 3, and 5 are sequentially higher, with intervening lower lows (points 2 and 4). The *signal* is the first daily close below the low of the day on which the market makes its highest high in creating point 5. The profit expectation is a retreat at least back to point 4, and often much lower, as in Figure 9.15.

I rethink the immediately pessimistic outlook derived from a Reverse Wave Sell on any daily close 1.67% over the high of point 5.

FIGURE 9.15 Reverse Wave Sell

Source: Chart courtesy of TCNet, a product of Worden Brothers, Inc. For more information, go to www.wataugamgt.com, and click on the hyperlink to TCNet. Graphic enhancements made by the author.

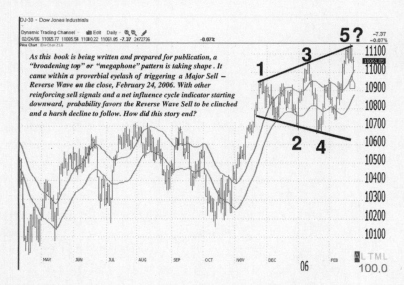

FIGURE 9.16 Major Sell—Reverse Wave, Pending in February 2006

Source: Chart courtesy of TCNet, a product of Worden Brothers, Inc. For more information, go to www.wataugamgt.com, and click on the hyperlink to TCNet. Graphic enhancements made by the author.

Students of the market should also play around with this pattern in other markets and other time frame charts, such as weekly, hourly, and even 15-minute bar charts. This pattern tends to repeat itself in many different time perspectives and, importantly, the trader/investor can place a stop-loss order a fractional percentage just above the high price of the high day *to minimize the risk of taking a contrarian position.*

MAJOR BUY-REVERSE WAVE

The *Reverse Wave pattern* works at intermediate-term market bottoms, too. The setup consists of sequentially lower lows, as *represented by points 1-3-5* in Figure 9.17, with intervening *higher highs* (i.e., points 2-4). This pattern is particularly helpful toward the end of trading range markets, so often leads to Continuation Buy signals that are harbingers of sustained advances, often exceeding normal boundaries of the upper band in our Dynamic Trading Channel.

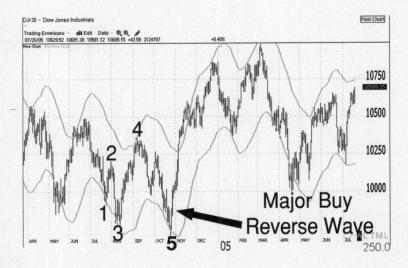

FIGURE 9.17 Reverse Wave Buy

Source: Chart courtesy of TCNet, a product of Worden Brothers, Inc. For more information, go to www.wataugamgt.com, and click on the hyperlink to TCNet. Graphic enhancements made by the author.

CONTINUATION SELL

Continuation Sell signals usually lead to a selling capitulation. I have three separate sets of market conditions that trigger a Continuation Sell, each equally powerful. When these occur, it is *better not to attempt establishing long positions until a Primary Buy is generated* in our system. Sometimes cycle work will suggest that a Continuation signal is probable. If, for example, we have gotten a Primary Sell near the highs, and the market declines (i.e., to the lower band of our Dynamic Trading Channel) followed by a lengthy consolidation period, then a Continuation Sell is especially probable if our net influence cycle study is pointing downward.

A Continuation Sell most often leads to selling capitulation, as shown in Figure 9.19, and is generally followed by a Primary Buy. In 1969, the selling capitulation phase was rather severe after the Continuation Sell in early June. The first Primary Buy in September 1969 was pretty good, but a little early. After a second Continuation Sell was generated in November 1969, including a more modest selling capitulation phase, a second Primary Buy in January 1970 led to a robust advance. In

FIGURE 9.18 Continuation Sell

Source: Chart courtesy of TCNet, a product of Worden Brothers, Inc. For more information, go to www.wataugamgt.com, and click on the hyperlink to TCNet. Graphic enhancements made by the author.

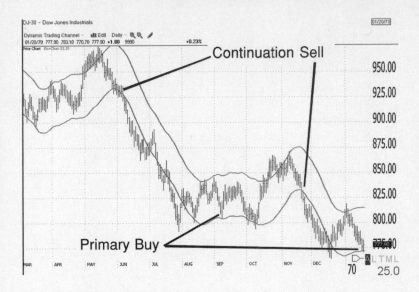

FIGURE 9.19   Continuation Sell

Source: Chart courtesy of TCNet, a product of Worden Brothers, Inc. For more information, go to www.wataugamgt.com, and click on the hyperlink to TCNet. Graphic enhancements made by the author.

backtesting our Primary Buy, the September 1969 was the only case in which an intermediate-term advance did not begin immediately.

CONTINUATION BUY

I have three different Continuation Buy signals, each with a distinct set of trigger criteria. What they all have in common is a high probability that a strong upside move will be extended, often one that crawls up the upper band of my Dynamic Trading Channel (similar to what is seen in Figure 9.10).

The Continuation Buy signal that occurred in early 1995 (Figure 9.21) was a classic instance where it led to a *very strong, immediate advance*. The market crawled up the upper band of my Dynamic Trading Channel for more than a 20% additional gain, exceeding my normal target range objective of a 4 to 16% extension from the point of the continuation signal. This demonstrated strength is one of the reasons why I give all benefit of doubt to the upside until my system generates a Major or Primary Sell.

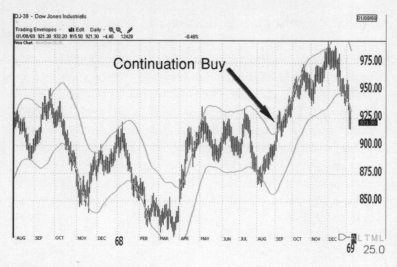

FIGURE 9.20 Continuation Buy

Source: Chart courtesy of TCNet, a product of Worden Brothers, Inc. For more information, go to www.wataugamgt.com, and click on the hyperlink to TCNet. Graphic enhancements made by the author.

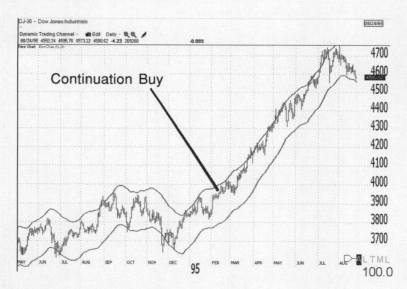

FIGURE 9.21 Continuation Buy in 1995

Source: Chart courtesy of TCNet, a product of Worden Brothers, Inc. For more information, go to www.wataugamgt.com, and click on the hyperlink to TCNet. Graphic enhancements made by the author.

PUTTING TIMING SIGNALS TO WORK

To take advantage of my market timing signals, Watauga Equity Management offers two mutual fund asset allocation services, *Index Plus* (moderate risk) and *Active Index* (aggressive risk). Two additional services, Sector Plus and Dynamic Trends, will be introduced in early summer, 2006. We also publish a periodic newsletter, *MarketView*, distributed only by e-mail. It is available by subscription, at a cost of $999 per year. It is also distributed free of charge to asset management clients who satisfy minimum account size requirements as a value-added service. Another application for timing skills is the development of a proprietary trading and investment fund, which I will consider.

ACT IV

MY MANAGEMENT SOLUTIONS

Back in 1983, I was a stockbroker with Rauscher Pierce Refsnes in San Diego. A new client of mine, a news editor for NBC Nightly News in Chicago, invited me back to the Windy City. While there, I took a tour of the Chicago Mercantile Exchange (CME), where stock index futures on the Standard & Poor's 500 Stock Index had begun trading barely a year earlier.

As I began trading the S&P futures in 1982, over the telephone I had talked with several of the futures professionals employed by Stotler & Co., the commodity brokerage that Rauscher Pierce then used. So this visit gave me an opportunity to put names with faces, and learn a little bit more about the futures game.

On the floor of the CME I watched and listened, and soon realized that the commodity people on the floor were largely treating the S&P like just about every other futures contract they had encountered, from soybeans to gold to currencies. Because of their next-to-nothing transaction costs, they were used to making money in the markets—a lot of money— by identifying a prevailing longer-term trend, up or down, then capturing a tick or two's profit on every trade. A "tick" is the contract's minimum fluctuation. In those days, a tick on each contract traded was worth $25. Buy and sell 100 times a day (profitably) for a tick, and you earned $2,500 per day. Do it 100 times for 10 contracts at a time instead of just one, and you made $25,000 per day. Average two ticks profit per trade for that kind of volume, and you make $50,000.

Understanding the commodity floor broker's business model of skimming the market time after time after time for one or two minimum fluctuations is one of the greatest lessons you can learn about how important today's low transaction costs are throughout the marketplace for publicly traded securities. Low transaction costs (commissions) allow for new and adapted investment and trading strategies compared to what Grandpa knew.

Of course, it wasn't a one-sided lesson on my visit to the floor. The commodity guys involved in stock index futures were eager to learn about how off-the-floor stock market guys plied their trade. Stotler's senior floor manager ushered me around the floor of the CME, pointing out this or that feature, all the while asking me questions about how I approached trading stock index futures. I have no idea whether he did this with all of his other guests on the floor, but after a while he said, "Tell me when to buy and I will buy a contract."

I said, "Are you serious?"

He replied, "Yes."

I told him, "If you are serious, stay close because you will have an opportunity within the next 10 minutes." He scratched his head in wonderment, but said, "Okay."

Unlike the floor brokers trading for a tick, I had much higher transaction costs ($100 per contract) in trading for customers off the floor. So instead of trading for $25 or $50 fluctuations, I needed to trade for $500 to $1,000 movements in the contract. We weren't really trading that differently, but my primary trends were several weeks in duration, whereas the floor trader's trend orientation might have been a few days, if not mere hours.

The S&P stock index in January 1983 was in a strong weekly uptrend. The March futures contract was already up 250 points that day, or $1,250 per contract. At the time, there were still daily limits of 500 points, which were rarely triggered. If a commodity market goes limit up or limit down, trading is effectively halted.

It was about 1:25 P.M. Central time when I told the Stotler floor manager to buy a March contract at the market. The market had been steadily retreating for about a half hour, down from a contract daily high near 47.20. He got a fill (his buy was executed) at 146.80, as I recall. Within about two minutes, the March contract was quoted at 146.65, a loss of three ticks, or $75 per contract.

The floor broker looked at me dead serious and asked, "Sell it, right, and cut my loss?"

"No," I replied.

"But I never lose more than $50 on a trade," he stated emphatically.

"But we aren't in this trade for $50," I said. "We're in it for at least $500."

"Oh," he said, doubtfully. Turning to a nearby order clerk, he said, "I don't want to lose any more than $200, so stop me out." And the order clerk nodded his understanding.

Five minutes later, the March S&P contract was trading higher, at the earlier daily high of 147.05, when the floor manager said, "Okay, now can I take profits?"

"No," I said. "Not yet."

"But I'm up $125 on this contract," he said. "And in less than 10 minutes!"

"I know," I answered. "But remember, this is not a $100 trade."

The floor manager, a 20+-year veteran of the commodity industry and an equity partner in Stotler, needed to know. "But when should I sell," he said, "if not now?"

I said, "Okay, if you need to know what we are shooting for, tell me what limit up is for the day."

"Why, 150.30," he stated. "But that's more than 200 points higher."

"Exactly," I said. "Put your sell order in for 150.25. I want to make sure you get out of this trade today."

Incredulously, he gave the sell instructions to the trader with the reminder, "Remember, I don't want to lose any more than $200."

Twenty-one minutes later, the March contract was trading limit up, at 150.30. The floor manager's sell order was executed at 150.25, and he pocketed a profit of about $1,225 on the contract. Still shaking his head as he shook my hand and said his thank-yous, he marveled, "Guys like you trading off the floor are changing this business."

One of the great things about the stock market is that the more you learn, the more you realize how much you still have to learn. For instance, even though I was a highly ranked futures "producer" for Rauscher Pierce, my naiveté was showing quite baldly because although that was a very profitable trade, a trading clerk on the floor pulled me aside later and advised me that I had cut off the profit by $25. "You could still have sold at limit up," she said. "You just can't do any more buying."

As a fledgling institutional research and sales guy in the 1990s, I was forever learning more from my customers and continue to learn today. One of the most piercing observations was by a San Francisco money manager in 1995, when he said, "Never mistake a bull market for brains."

There are many different investment and trading approaches, and many can be successful in different market environments. As my San Francisco friend suggested, a bull market can make a lot of very marginally conceived investment strategies and stock selection methods look pretty good. But it is when the overall market is in a corrective period that the rubber meets the road, so to speak.

Grandpa didn't have too many choices in dealing with corrective periods. In fact, he was too busy "buying good companies" to care. But investors today have so many more choices, and in such a very different structural environment.

Qualified retirement plans allow for shorter-term repositioning of assets without concern for tax liabilities. Low commission costs facilitate off-the-floor, short-term trading strategies previously executable only by floor traders and exchange members. And the traditional "buyer of good companies" can neutralize the potential impact of an adverse, corrective market period without having to commit additional capital and without having to sell the prized "steeds" he has chosen to run in the stock market performance race.

In this section, I outline my personal preferences for management strategies using the overall stock market's influence on performance. They are designed to better manage risk while prospectively enhancing returns. Are they the very best strategies? Probably not, but they are the best for me. Are there others out there? Of course.

But these solutions make sense to me, with my skill set, my resources, my risk tolerance, and my investment objectives—my investment and trading personality. While examining mine, I invite you to consider your own pursuit of superior results instead of accepting the guaranteed mediocre and sub-par performances that are shoved down our throats by most of the financial services industry.

10

My Mutual Fund Asset Allocation Solutions

Through my investment advisory firm, Watauga Equity Management, I currently offer two mutual fund asset allocation services, with two more soon to be introduced.

INDEX PLUS—MODEST RISK

Index Plus is the evolved manifestation of my original interest in employing mutual fund timing strategies, dating back to 1984 and the Kemper Investment Portfolios fund family. I have engaged the basic principles, off and on for family and friends, ever since. Since the early 1990s, producing and selling research to the institutional investment community was my primary business interest, so I have only been continuously engaged in mutual fund *active allocation* strategies since late 2002. Theta Research, the previously mentioned performance analytics firm based in Philadelphia, has tracked Index Plus since then.

The basic strategy of Index Plus is to use my timing signals for the overall market to commit client capital to a modestly leveraged stock index fund position during highly probable rising markets, and switching capital to cash (money market), to protect principal and previously earned profits during adverse or corrective market periods.

Index Plus uses the Rydex Dynamic Dow fund and the Rydex Government Money Market fund. We adjust our capital allocations so that long positions have a 1.50× relationship to the Dow Industrials, so they are moderately leveraged. With a 1.50× relationship, if the Dow Industrials advance 10% then our accounts should advance approximately 15%. While the Rydex Dynamic funds have slightly higher expense ratios than some of the other Rydex index funds, we like the flexibility of having both morning and afternoon fund pricings. Also, there are certain times when we will commit a maximum amount of capital to equity exposure, with full leverage.

With experience, you learn that risk is not necessarily limited to the two-dimensional concept taught by the buy-and-hold traditionalists that also taught our grandfathers. They assert that concentrating assets in one stock or a very few industry sectors or a single asset class (stocks, as opposed to bonds) represents risk. And they teach us that the use of leverage represents risk. But very few teach us directly about the third dimension of risk: timing. Sure, most traditional, long-only portfolio managers are concerned with relative valuation in the stocks they buy, but they don't baldly base their decisions on the timing component of risk in investing in their good companies (at least most don't admit to it, anyway).

So while traditional academicians and investment practitioners may differ with me, I place Timing right up there with Leverage and Asset Concentration on the pedestal of equally important risks. The challenge, of course, is that you have to master timing skills, and in ignorance most people disdain the notion that the market *can* be timed.

As documented by Theta Research, the compounded annual growth rate (CAGR) of Index Plus has been approximately 11.14% after fees over the past 36 months ending April 23, 2006, in spite of an admittedly challenging period for us during the first quarter of 2005. When you consider that we were only in the market and so *exposed to equity risk just 49% of the time*, that's decent investment performance. Our standard deviation over the three-year period is roughly 10%, versus a total return of 37.27%.

It's important to understand that evaluating performance at different points in time will return different results. As this is being written in late April 2006, Index Plus has been in money market for several weeks as our research points to an uncertain period just ahead, and potentially a harsh market decline. So we want to protect principal and previously earned profits and are willing to give up any remaining upside. But as recently as mid-February, the same calculation of trailing 36-month performance was a compounded rate of return of a little more than 15%, so the several weeks of just earning money market interest lowers the CAGR accordingly.

Different market periods will produce different results, too. While Index Plus performance was flat to slightly down in calendar year 2005, reflecting a challenging year for the overall market generally, in calendar 2004 the Index Plus return was +24.4% after fees, nearly three times (3×) the 8.99% return of the S&P 500 and just about four times (4×) the less than 6% return of the Dow Industrials. Through March 31, 2006, the year-to-date performance was 4.38% (a little more than 16% annualized, but we will need [1] a rising market at some point in the year, and [2] a good and timely entry point for getting on board that rising market early, as well as a timely exit if such an advance falters, for us to see a 16% or better annual return).

ACTIVE INDEX–AGGRESSIVE RISK

Our *Active Index* timing service uses the same timing model as Index Plus, but we use a more aggressive equity exposure during forecasted advancing markets. The most important distinguishing characteristic, however, is that when corrective or declining markets are considered probable, then we will commit money in Active Index to leveraged *inverse* equity index funds that increase in value as the overall market declines. During the three-year period ending April 23, 2006, Active Index was 100% invested in money market approximately 39% of the time.

As of April 23, 2006, the compounded average annual rate of return for Active Index over the past 36 months was 18.20%, after management fees, according to Theta Research. The same calculation in mid-February showed approximately a 25% compounded average annual rate of return. In calendar 2004, our Active Index performance after fees was 29.17%, almost triple the performance of the S&P 500. On May 25, 2006, our year-to-date performance was approximately 14.50% after fees, or a little more than 40% annualized. But in order to get something near or better than that annualized return we have to show good timing for the rest of the year!

SECTOR PLUS–MODERATE RISK

Sector Plus is a new service that we are introducing in the early summer of 2006, based on the concept previously mentioned in this book that one way to achieve superior investment results is to focus on individual industry groups. The Rydex family of mutual funds includes 19 sector funds, all of which are candidates for our capital commitments. The funds include Banking, Basic Materials, Biotechnology, Commodities, Consumer Products, Electronics, Energy, Energy Services, Financial Services, Health Care, Internet, Leisure, Precious Metals, Real Estate, Retailing, Technology, Telecommunications, Transportation, and Utilities.

Our decision-making process utilizes a combined fundamental and technical approach. The technical methods identify contrarian-oriented accumulation patterns over three different time frames: short-, intermediate-, and long-term. The long-term accumulation pattern is especially important, because our aim is to anticipate key reversal points in intermediate-term sector trends. Once we identify a promising sector for reversal, we evaluate the fundamental and macroeconomic factors that might contribute to the sector's gaining favor in the weeks and months ahead. Generally, we anticipate having capital commitments to no more than five industry groups at a time.

The "Plus" in this service is that when we anticipate a severe decline for the overall stock market, we may reduce the long capital exposure in each industry sector by up to 25%, and commit those funds to inverse equity index funds, such as the Rydex Inverse Dynamic Dow fund. We may also commit up to 25% of available capital into a leveraged, broad index fund like Rydex Dynamic Dow fund or Rydex Nova.

DYNAMIC TREND—AGGRESSIVE RISK

Dynamic Trend is another new program we are introducing, and it is quite a departure from the contrary opinion–derived methods we have historically used. This active asset allocation service is conceptually constructed to latch full force onto strongly trending markets, up or down, with full leverage, but to minimize the whipsaw uncertainty of consolidating market periods.

This service will always be fully invested, with capital commitments to long or short funds at Rydex derived from the S&P 500, the Dow Jones Industrials, the NASDAQ 100, and the S&P Midcap 400. Other potential indexes will also be considered.

11

My Convergence Fund Solution

This chapter provides greater detail on how I see the rigors of long-only, traditional portfolio management converging with the flexibility of proprietary investment and trading funds, coloquially known as hedge funds.

In constructing my hedge fund solution, I felt it was important to establish some very clear objectives to satisfy the several constituent interests, especially the prospective institutional investor in the fund.

First, the regulatory environment demands an ever-growing need for disclosure and transparency, so in anticipation of increased regulatory attention to hedge funds we want to pursue investment and trading strategies that are *not adversely affected by transparency*. All trading and investment positions will be expediently reported, and are not compromised in any way by broader public knowledge. This is especially important, too, because much of the future capital provided to hedge funds will come from institutional investors, such as pension and retirement systems, and insurance companies. While they don't necessarily need to know all of the research and trading secrets, they need to have a general idea of the strategies in which they are risking capital. *Transparency and disclosure are neces-*

sary components of the investment and trading model if substantial amounts of institutional capital is sought.

Because I want my fund to have institutional appeal, bringing significant amounts of capital under management, then whatever investment and trading strategies that are employed must be *highly scalable*. This rules out the sort of illiquid strategies and vehicles in which many hedge funds today find market inefficiencies to exploit.

Finally, the institutional investor is less inclined to invest with hedge fund management companies that are dependent on single individuals, a major concern for me. So I need plans to share market knowledge with key employees as I build the infrastructure of my management company. Not only does that mean having adequate noncompete and nondisclosure agreements in place, but also a compensation plan that will discourage key employees from migrating to other firms or starting their own.

Ideally, the hedge fund model will have a high probability of producing consistently profitable returns. They don't have to be out-of-this-world great, but well above average over time.

Finally, the hedge fund compensation structure should be fair. Given the more competitive atmosphere in the hedge fund industry to attract capital, managers will have to reassess what is fair considering who is taking the capital risk and their investment models return expectations.

My hedge fund management model is simple, straightforward, and very much in keeping with the principles outlined in *The 90% Solution*. In fact, I have a feeling that my model represents the future convergence of the traditional long-only management styles widely practiced today and the more aggressive hedge fund styles that are currently successful in attracting assets. As discussed earlier, this convergence has already begun. Traditional managers are beginning to realize they have to do something to differentiate themselves from all of the closet indexers in the marketplace. And the hedge fund industry is becoming more sophisticated and faces increasing competition as it tries to enter the mainstream.

My model includes:

- Establish long-only positions in individual equities, unleveraged, using well-defined stock selection methods.
- On overall market timing sell signals, *neutralize* the market's potential adverse impact by using the marginability of the long equity portfolio to sell equity index ETFs against the portfolio.

- On overall market buy signals, cover any short sales in equity index ETFs and use up to one-third of the long portfolio's marginability to execute naked sales of ETF put option contracts or to purchase long positions in ETFs.

The long-only portfolio will be subdivided into four distinct selection strategies:

1. Emerging Growth (30% of assets)
   - Small and mid-cap companies with products or technologies that represent a structural change in the way we live and do business.
   - Small and mid-cap companies with a value proposition.
   - Two-year appreciation target of at least 100%.
2. Core Growth (30%)
   - Large cap.
   - Brand name products and services.
   - Essential products and services.
   - Not a question of whether they are great companies, but when to commit to the long-term growth trend.
   - Some option writing.
   - Two-year appreciation target of at least 50%.
3. Sector Focus (20%)
   - Large and mid-cap.
   - Commitments to major industry trends (i.e., energy, health care, interest rates, commodities, real estate, technology).
4. Powertrends (20%)
   - Small and mid-cap.
   - Technically derived selection and liquidations.

I feel this model is scalable to at least $5 billion under management, perhaps more. It is important to note that even though the overall stock market's direction may explain up to 90% or more of a well-diversified portfolio's performance, making investment decisions for long stock positions and when to sell ETFs against the portfolio represent two separate strategies. Selling ETFs is not a pure hedge, no matter how much the overall market explains a diversified portfolio's performance. So not only must each stock selection be independently monitored and evaluated, but the market timing system for buying and selling ETFs must be reviewed separately, too, for its on-going efficacy.

This investment model uses superior stock selection methods, thus increasing the probability that the long portfolio will be comprised of good companies in each of the four categories. But it also uses a proven and powerful market timing system not only to neutralize the potential adverse impact of corrective or declining market periods, but also to enhance returns during rising overall market periods. And, importantly, the exciting upside potential of the individual stock selections is left unhindered by the market neutralization strategies.

Finally, because this model is highly scalable, I want to attract large amounts of institutional capital. Sophisticated investors will find the model more appealing if it features a fair consideration of who is taking the capital risk. Consequently, my firm's compensation structure will not be the typical "2 and 20" fee plan charged by so many hedge funds (2% annual management fee versus 20% of new profits). Rather, we are more likely to charge something closer to a 1% annual management fee versus 10% of new appreciation.

My bet is that by not departing too terribly much from what the institutions are already investing trillions of dollars in; by promising to enhance returns and better manage risk through rather simple, easy-to-understand strategies; and by constructing an important balance in the compensation schedule between asset size and incentives, several institutional investors interested in earning superior returns will at least give us an audience.

OTHER APPROACHES

Through the years, I have made many friends in both the traditional and alternative investment segments of the money management and stock market research industries. I think my work stacks up pretty well, but I am not the only smart guy. Moreover, there are many who have contributed to my learning. This section provides a little more insight into my approaches to the market timing and investing processes, but more specifically focuses on those who have been research mentors along the way and on those who offer what I perceive to be value-added timing or investment resources. There are many others that I *could* have included, but these are the most important that come to mind.

12

Broad Strokes

Different investors have different time and risk perspectives. In fact, the very first thing I advise people to do when considering the use of a new indicator or research tool, or a decision-making aid such as a newsletter, is to make sure that their time perspective matches the time horizon of the indicator, tool, or decision-making aid.

Many years ago, when I was first starting out, I learned this the hard way. I was doing very short-term trading of options and index futures. A couple of newsletters to which I was subscribing mentioned the importance of a glaring divergence in the number of new highs on the New York Stock Exchange as the market averages were going to new highs. The implications, the newsletter writers said, were extremely bearish—and they gave some very persuasive historical examples. So being the good student of history that I am, I started selling short index futures and buying put options to capitalize on my good fortune at having read this material.

Well, I broke what has since become my cardinal rule (which I didn't know back then): Always match the time perspectives of the decision-making tool with your trading or investment strategy. We were in the last stage of a strong, intermediate-term market advance and, as it turned out, the type of divergences the newsletters were identifying could last for several weeks, if not months before prices turned decisively down. They were early warning signs, to be sure, but hardly useful for short-term trading purposes. The education was effective, probably because it was expensive!

Many of this book's readers have neither the time nor the inclination to develop a timing methodology that fits my time perspective, which is more intermediate-term oriented. That is, my decisions about the overall market's direction are for 3- to 18-month trends. While I consider this to be the optimum time perspective for maximizing return and minimizing risk, and still allowing room for occasional errors in judgment, many investors would regard that time perspective as frenetic. Day traders, of course, would consider my time perspective to be way too laid-back for their needs.

So I want to open this final section of the book by introducing readers to a couple of other professionals' timing approaches that I regard as pretty good, even if they do not match my perceived optimization perspective. I don't have a monopoly on good ideas or good timing skills. What is right for me is not necessarily appropriate for someone else.

For investors who want to take a longer-term timing approach, which I call a *broad strokes* approach, I recommend familiarizing yourself with the work of **Bob Brinker**, author/editor of *Bob Brinker's Marketimer*, the work of **Richard Russell**, author/editor of *Dow Theory Letters*, and the work of **George Muzea**, author/editor of *The Magic T*.

Brinker, based in Castle Rock, Colorado, hosts Money Talk, a popular personal finance talk show that reaches a nationwide audience, in addition to writing his newsletter. He epitomizes what I call a "broad strokes timer," because he makes very few calls and has very reasoned fundamental and macroeconomic explanations for his current opinion. As I am writing this section in early March 2006, Brinker's current issue of *Marketimer* discusses the effects of (1) tight money; (2) rising (interest) rates; (3) high inflation; (4) rapid growth; and (5) overvaluation. He summarizes by saying that "the five root causes of a bear market are not indicating that a new cyclical bear market is likely at this time. On the contrary," he says, "we see an economy that continues to grow at a sustainable and moderate pace, a Federal Reserve that is getting close to the end of its rate tightening cycle in advance of the November elections, core inflation that remains benign, and a valuation level that offers the potential for a continuation of the cyclical bull market."

Whether or not you agree with him on all counts (I don't very often), he has a very thoughtful and thought-provoking approach for putting his timing model into fundamental perspective. He writes in a lucid, plain-English style, and at $185 per year, provides information and understanding about the markets and the economy that students of the stock market should want to acquire.

Here is Bob Brinker's contact information:

Bob Brinker
Marketimer
858 Happy Canyon Road, Suite 255
Castle Rock, Colorado, 80108
303-660-8686
web site: www.bobbrinker.com

Richard Russell has become one of the most widely read newsletter writers of our time, and is the latest in a long line of Dow Theory adherents that began when Charles H. Dow began publishing the *Wall Street Journal* in 1889 and included small editorials containing his theories. In public sections of his web site, www.dowtheoryletters.com, Russell writes, "The Dow Theory (actually it is a set of observations) has basically to do with buying great values and selling those values when they become overpriced.

"Value is the operative word in Dow Theory," Russell continues. "All other Dow Theory considerations are secondary to the value thesis. Therefore, price action, support lines, resistance, confirmations, divergence—all are of much less importance than value considerations, although critics of the Theory seem totally unaware of that fact."

Russell credits William P. Hamilton, Robert Shea, and E. George Schaefer for preceding him in the advance of The Dow Theory principles. What I like about Russell's approach is *his emphasis on perceiving value*, accumulating value at low prices, and selling value at high prices. Even if his broad strokes approach does not fit with my personal reward/risk optimization perspective, his patient orientation toward value perception is dead on the mark. If you do nothing else, go to his web site and read the series of essays that are publicly available under "Popular Articles."

Richard Russell's contact information is:

Richard Russell
Dow Theory Letters, Inc.
P O Box 1759
La Jolla, California 92038-1759
858-454-0481
e-mail: staff@dowtheoryletters.com
web site: www.dowtheoryletters.com

In addition to Russell and Brinker, I find the broad strokes of **George Muzea**'s "Magic T" methodology an interesting read. Author of the book, *The Vital Few vs. the Trivial Many: Invest with the Insiders, Not the Masses* (Hoboken, NJ: John Wiley & Sons, 2005), Muzea gauges the investment activities of those he considers "the vital few," insiders, against the activities of those he considers the "the trivial many." The latter category includes sections he refers to as "Advisory Sentiment," "State of the Market," "Mood of the Media," and "Mood of Friends and Acquaintances."

I don't have subscription costs, but his contact information is:

George Muzea
Muzea Advisors
5920 Lausanne Drive
Reno, Nevada, 89511
775-849-1550
e-mail: gmuzea@charter.net
web site: www.georgemunzea.com

13

Other Timing Approaches and Resources

If you really think about it, the conceptual approach to timing the market is pretty simple. Buy low. Sell high. Or, increase your *long* exposure to stocks at perceived overall market bottoms and increase your hedged, cash, or short sale exposure at predicted overall market tops.

Of course, it isn't quite that simple. *No one really predicts market turns, whatever they might say. If they claim to, they are lying to you and to themselves.*

Instead, they are establishing the *probability* of future market direction based on comparing then-current market circumstances to historical observations of market patterns and circumstances that seem to repeat themselves, whether derived from fundamental, technical, cyclical, quantitative, astrological, divine providence, or some other methodology.

That is not to say that market events can't be influenced. I suspect, for example, without any way of actually knowing, that Osama bin Laden and his cronies were executing short sales and liquidating long positions in U.S. stocks before September 11, 2001. *I observed intense distribution occurring among stocks—and among the overall market averages—in my proprietary technical studies before those tragic events.* Most bothersome was that these distribution patterns just did not make a lot of sense at the time, because except for some Internet stocks beginning to falter, the economic world seemed to be in fairly good shape. *Somebody knew something*, we look back and suspect with the benefit of 20/20 hindsight. (See Figure 13.1.)

There are few people in the civilized world that could have imagined such a sinister attack on a civilian target. We just aren't used to thinking that way. *From the beginning of the Dow Industrial's toppy pattern beginning in the early spring of 1999, there was evidence of corrective forces in the marketplace. Valuations were, indeed, obscenely high.* Internet stocks began to crater in early 2000, but while the Dow Industrials had periods of briefly sharp declines, the non-Internet sectors seemed to be holding up fairly well. After two years of mostly consolidating equity prices, *it was*

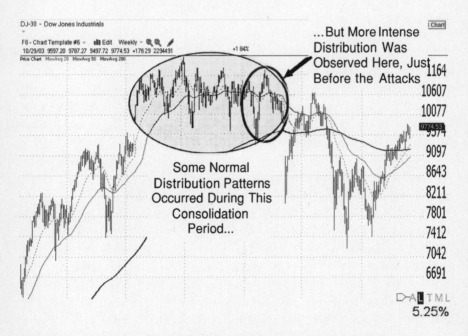

FIGURE 13.1   Distribution Patterns before September 11, 2001

Source: Chart courtesy of TCNet, a product of Worden Brothers, Inc. For more information, go to www.wataugamgt.com, and click on the hyperlink to TCNet. Graphic enhancements made by the author.

easy to speculate by the summer of 2001 that the stock market averages might soon stage another meaningful advance.

But it was not to be. I don't really know if Bin Laden had executed short sales in stocks going into 9/11. I am not aware of any market guru who publicly predicted in the summer of 2001 that an overall stock market decline would soon be forthcoming because of a terrorist attack on the World Trade Center.

Even today I still mourn and remember the people who died so needlessly, including many business and rugby friends from my days living and working in New York City. *But beyond the needless and tragic loss of human life, 9/11 threw a monkey wrench in the whole economy.* People simply stopped much of their business activity. People stopped traveling. Airplanes quit flying. Increased security measures everywhere put additional pressures on the expense side of corporate income statements, particularly among those large companies engaged in global business. I am pretty sure there is neither a technical nor fundamental-derived forecasting system in the world that predicted this would happen.

Whether it is my work or someone else's, we really can only aspire to *identify moments in time where there is increased probability* that the market will go up or down. To achieve this implies that you create a system or *timing model.* If it is a true system, you have based your model on historical pattern observations that engender a favored scenario—if all works according to probability, then what direction the market will go, and within what time frame. Beyond that, your system must have caveats: If the favored scenario doesn't pan out, what do you do if such and such happens, and *how do you rethink your expectations and strategies* if some other pattern unexpectedly materializes.

While everyone may have an opinion about what the market might do, there are a relative few who are confident enough to put their neck on the line and put it in writing, document at least a vague reason why, and give you some idea of when he or she will admit to being in error. Even better than putting it in writing (i.e., newsletters) is taking responsibility for the asset management and having your compensation structured so that you have the proper incentives not only to earn profits on the capital entrusted to you, but also to protect principal. That's why I have the greatest amount of respect for almost all money managers, especially those engaged in active portfolio management. Even if they are nothing more than closet indexers, they put their skill sets and reputations on the line every single day and are judged quarterly for their respective performances.

I did an Internet search on Google this afternoon (February 20, 2006) for "stock market timing" to get a sense of other resources that might be available to an investor wanting to use an outside money manager focused on overall market timing, or a newsletter-type subscription service to develop a do-it-yourself timing model. *I got 19.3 million results!* So I narrowed my search, looking for "overall stock market timing," and still got *9.81 million* results. Not only does everybody seem to have an opinion about market direction, they may have three of them!

In reality, there are an increasing number of people in the investment world who are waking up to the importance of overall stock market direction and trying to capitalize. I doubt anyone has the time and energy to screen 9 million potential sources for style and substance, but I encourage people to develop their own timing model or system, because *as you develop ownership of it, and understand its strengths (and flaws), you will eventually be more successful* with its implementation. If you stay with it through the trial-and-error, developmental phase, the system or methodology will reflect *your* investment personality, *your* tolerance for risk, *your* investment objectives, and *your* available resources.

Most people, however, are simply overwhelmed by the academic challenge. They don't break down the psychological processes involved with Fear, Greed, and Valuation. They don't grasp that the markets ebb and flow, constantly, in a series of overreactions of investor sentiment above and below some intangible, but very real "value line." Greed drives prices higher and higher, until the "market gods", or the Smart Money investors, look down and say, "Hey, intrinsic value, or the 'real' value of stocks is way back down there." So they start selling. Fear feeds upon itself, snowballing into a selling avalanche until one day Smart Money investors look upward and say, "Hey, the intrinsic value, or the 'real' value of stocks is way back up there." So they start buying. And the process repeats itself, over and over and over again.

I offer five key suggestions to anyone aspiring to time the stock market:

1. *The majority doesn't rule.* The market exists to *fool the vast majority of people* as many times as possible. Human beings are emotional animals, so the market achieves its goal most of the time. *By the time most people jump on the bandwagon, the market is often ready to go the other*

direction. Especially to this point, George Muzea ("The Magic T") has it right. Few people are brave enough to go against the crowd. They are jump-on-the-bandwagon trend followers. The "trivial many," he says, don't get excited about stocks until near a market top. So when stocks are the hottest topic at every cocktail party, it's probably time to think about selling, or at least hedging your positions.

2. *Take it with a grain of salt.* The *financial media are the absolute worst communication vehicle* from which to receive information about the overall stock market, at least information that might lead to a sound investment decision. There are scant few of the "talking heads" worth listening to. I listen to Larry Kudlow on CNBC whenever I want to explain why the stock market *should* go up, because Mr. Kudlow seems doggedly bullish, and as far as I can tell, he is doggedly bullish on life and business in America nearly all of the time. His faith in market-driven economic systems is laudable, and his optimism is contagious. David Faber strikes me as one of the most informed journalists on *individual* stocks to ever attach a microphone to his lapel (or wherever they attach them now). The same can be said of Joe Kernen, especially on healthcare issues. Becky Quick is refreshingly straightforward and unassuming in her reporting. Mark Haines has a cynicism that is genuinely disarming, like he knows our collective pain. While I don't always agree with his assessment, Steve Liesman is not afraid to offer some interesting insights on the economy (and he even took the time to answer my e-mail to him once!). I also like listening to Erin Burnett, Ron Insana, and Carl Quintanilla for their sometimes incisive questions and comments.

But as good as they are, there isn't one of these TV journalists that will help you time the overall market's direction, and each of them will probably be the first to admit that issuing such missives is not in their mission statement. In general, *all journalists tend to get caught up in the fervor of what just happened, or is happening.* Listen to what they are all saying, just to stay in tune with the times, but *don't* try to base any market timing decision on what they have to say.

3. *Play by the rules.* Creating a system implies that you have developed a set of rules by which to invest or trade. These *guidelines to live by are generally based on your well-studied recognition of historical patterns or circumstances that repeat themselves*—and that *probably* will result in a subsequent similar pattern or set of market circumstances. Your rules al-

low you to *act confidently, without emotion.* If such and such happens, then I get a buy signal. If the market does this while breadth does that, I get a sell signal. And (very important) if the market does not respond the way I expect it to within a certain amount of time, then I have to either exit the position or be willing to give it additional time to work out. If I choose the latter, then I must be willing to accept the additional risk and potentially increased adverse consequences. *If I can't play by the rules of my system, then I should not be participating in the game because I will either drive myself nuts-or to bankruptcy.*

4. *Good timing tools are generally universal.* Almost every good stock market decision-making tool is valid in nearly every kind of market and in many different time frames. Sure, there are nuances to be considered when applying an effective tool for trading pork bellies to the market for trading the QQQQs. Maybe you use a shorter or longer moving average. Or maybe your parameters for one market, or a certain time frame, are different.

But the only real exception to this principle is when data is not available for one market that is available for another. For example, many of us use technical analysis tools based on stock market breadth (e.g., the difference between the number of daily advancing stocks vs. the number of declining stocks), but the same sort of corresponding data may not be available for heating oil futures or other commodity contracts.

But especially in using technical analysis, a market is a market is a market. Study the action, not whether it is the SPY exchange-traded fund, the common stock of Cisco Systems, or soybean futures. And very often, *many of the same principles or rules will be as applicable to 15-minute bar charts as to weekly bar charts.*

5. *What is the time perspective?* Invariably, new users of technical analysis tools get excited when they read somewhere about somebody who made an important timing decision based on such and such indicator. So they try it—and it doesn't work for them.

Sure, certain technical tools may be entirely useless, just like some elements of fundamental analysis have little decision-making value. But the most common reason any technical indicator fails to add value is because the investor/trader is making decisions for a different time horizon than for what the tool is intended. I made this mistake personally in my early years. It's also important to know that not every indicator or signal works every time. That's why we are only establishing probability, not predicting. And you have to have an exit strategy.

I want to share with my readers a *few resources and even methodologies outside of my own that I consider especially useful.*

TIGER SOFTWARE AND PEERLESS SYSTEMS

Dr. William ("Bill") Schmidt, Ph.D., is the founder and developer of Peerless, an overall market timing system based on his well-documented technical analysis methodologies. His other product is Tiger, which performs his proprietary technical analysis and rankings on individual stocks. (See Figure 13.2, for an example on the OEX.)

I have known Bill since 1982, when I was working in San Diego and became one of his very first customers after he developed and wrote the Peerless and Tiger software applications. In the early years, it only ran on the Apple II+ computer (IBM-based PCs weren't around yet), so by today's standards the downloading of data and processing the analysis were agonizingly slow. Back in those days, I remember that with his Tiger software for individual stocks, you could keep 250 days' worth of data for just 27 stocks on each 5-1/4″ floppy disk. For option trading purposes, I followed 105 companies, so had 5 disks to update and process every night. I recall that I could

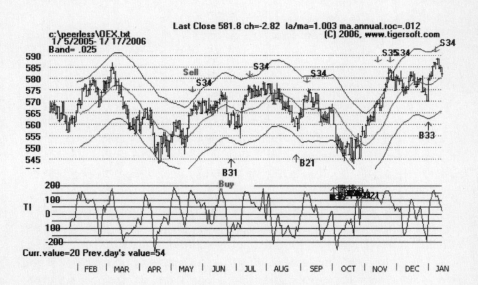

FIGURE 13.2 Sample Peerless/Tiger Chart with Automatic Signals
Source: Copyright 2006, www.tigersoft.com.

not begin the download until after 6:00 P.M. The downloading, processing, and graphing process (remember the slow dot-matrix printers?) took me three to four hours every evening. Then I had to be back at the office *by 5:30 A.M. the next day to prepare for the stock market's 6:30 A.M. opening!*

Thankfully, the advances in computer technology over the last 25 years have led to markedly increased productivity when it comes to market information and analysis. Today's *Tiger software now allows you to download, analyze, and rank over four times as many stocks—generating several times more information about each stock—all within about five minutes.*

But, *for this book, it is the Peerless system for overall market timing in which we are most interested.* If you do nothing else in developing a market timing system, to purchase the Peerless software is as good a beginning as I could recommend. *Roughly a third of my own market timing research is based on concepts and principles I learned from the Peerless system.*

For a system that takes very little time to update and not very much effort to run, and that gives you *automatic* intermediate-term buy and sell signals that are actionable, the Peerless system has a pretty good track record (see Table 13.1). *For the Dow Jones Industrial Average, over the last 40 years for which Dr. Schmidt has compiled and back-tested data, the system has generated 117 trades (an average of about three per year), 81% of which were profitable. The average profit per trade has been 8.49% and the average yearly gain about 25.5% (unleveraged).*

This particular system is *always in the market.* If someone had taken every signal, and either bought or sold short the Dow Industrials at the indicated prices (actual prices on the next day's opening would vary slightly, for or against), then *a $500 investment in 1965 compounds to approximately $3,609,076 through September 20, 2005.*

I personally know that the signals since 1982 have been real, not hypothetical. The one caveat to that statement is that he has developed and added some signals over the past 20 years. Anything numbered higher than a B12 or S12 has been added (and of course back-tested) to produce the track record shared below.

In Table 13.1, it is assumed that all positions are reversed (long to short, and vice versa) on every trade. For example, the DJI Close for the Sell S12 signal for January 6, 1966 is the closing trade value for the just previous Buy B18 signal. In addition, the same Sell S12 signal price close is also the opening price for a short sale position that was held to August 30, 1966. The compounded investment results (the return on $500) assumes that no money is paid out of the account for either short- or long-term capital gains tax liabilities that might have been incurred.

TABLE 13.1 Peerless Intermediate-Term Signals for Dow Industrials Since 1965

Date		Signals B=Buy S=Sell	Close	Percent Gain	$500 Investment Compounded
1965	09/24	B18	929.54	6.02%	gain on long trade $530
1966	01/06	S12	985.46	21.28%	gain on short sale $643
1966	8/30	B1	975.72	4.97%	$675
1966	9/15	S12	814.03	2.37%	$691
1966	11/22	B9	794.98	9.41%	$756
1967	03/17	S12	869.77	2.54%	$775
1967	04/11	B19	847.66	4.70%	$812
1967	04/24	S12	887.53	1.46%	$823
1967	05/19	B9	874.55	6.28%	$875
1967	09/14	S12	929.44	6.21%	$929
1968	01/22	B9	871.71	6.20%	$987
1969	01/07	S10	925.72	28.36%	$1,267
1970	05/27	B12/B19	663.2	9.08%	$1,382
1970	07/16	S12	723.44	1.51%	$1,403
1970	08/11	B9	712.55	9.40%	$1,535
1970	11/11	S12	779.5	−5.15%	$1,456
1970	12/15	B4	819.62	9.79%	$1,598
1971	08/17	S9/S12	899.9	7.62%	$1,720
1971	11/30	B12	831.34	15.41%	$1,985
1972	04/06	S9	959.44	2.71%	$2,039
1972	05/03	B20	933.47	3.41%	$2,108
1972	05/22	S12	965.31	5.55%	$2,225
1972	7/18	B20	911.72	4.39%	$2,323
1972	8/04	S12	951.76	2.66%	$2,384
1972	10/17	B20	926.48	12.66%	$2,687
1973	01/03	S9	1,043.8	9.89%	$2,953
1973	09/25	B4	940.55	4.94%	$3,098
1973	10/26	S9	987.06	16.07%	$3,596
1974	02/07	B9	828.46	4.50%	$3,758
1974	04/19	S9	865.77	29.82%	$4,879
1974	10/07	B19	607.56	35.57%	$6,709
1975	08/29	S12	835.34	0.75%	$6,759

(Continued)

TABLE 13.1   *(Continued)*

Date		Signals B=Buy S=Sell	Close	Percent Gain	$500 Investment Compounded
1975	12/04	B9	829.11	19.85%	gain on long trade $8,100
1976	03/09	S12	993.70	2.21%	gain on short sale $8,280
1976	05/25	B20	971.69	−7.04	$7,696
1977	05/25	S10	903.24	10.66%	$8,517
1977	12/06	B9	806.91	−2.77%	$8,281
1978	01/09	S10	784.56	4.28%	$8,636
1978	02/23	B9	750.95	11.73%	$9,649
1978	07/17	S12	839.05	−5.70%	$9,099
1978	08/03	B4	886.87	0.54%	$9,148
1978	10/10	S9/S12	891.63	7.16%	$9,803
1978	11/01	B19	827.79	7.99%	$10,587
1979	09/21	S9	893.94	9.68%	$11,611
1979	11/21	B9	807.42	7.15%	$12,442
1980	01/06	S12	865.19	10.12%	$13,701
1980	03/28	B19	777.65	28.61%	$17,621
1980	11/20	S12	1,000.17	6.61%	$18,786
1980	12/09	B17	934.04	4.15%	$19,566
1981	01/02	S9/S12	972.78	2.73%	$20,099
1981	01/21	B9	946.25	2.17%	$20,536
1981	02/26	S9	966.81	12.85%	$23,175
1981	09/28	B19	842.56	−2.10%	$22,689
1982	07/12	S9	824.87	−0.77%	$22,513
1982	08/17	B12	831.24	29.45%	$29,144
1983	01/07	S12	1,076.07	4.27%	$30,387
1983	01/24	B9	1,030.17	17.15%	$35,598
1983	09/01	S9	1,206.81	−2.99%	$34,534
1984	01/24	B9	1,242.88	−3.69%	$33,260
1984	02/03	S10	1,197.03	5.41%	$35,061
1984	04/06	B10	1,132.22	4.48%	$36,630
1984	05/01	S12	1,182.89	4.15%	$38,150
1984	05/18	B20	1,133.79	19.49%	$45,585
1985	10/14	S9	1,354.73	−6.30%	$42,715
1985	11/18	B4	1,440.02	10.63%	$47,256
1986	02/05	S9	1,593.12	−2.09%	$46,269

TABLE 13.1 *(Continued)*

Date		Signals B=Buy S=Sell	Close	Percent Gain	$500 Investment Compounded
1986	02/10	B4	1,626.38	14.57%	gain on long trade $53,009
1986	06/04	S9	1,863.29	2.00%	gain on short sale $54,068
1986	07/09	B9	1,826.07	0.52%	$54,347
1986	08/12	S9	1,835.49	2.32%	$55,609
1986	09/11	B17	1,792.89	33.32%	$74,139
1987	04/03	S9	2,390.34	4.49%	$77,470
1987	04/15	B19	2,282.95	2.59%	$79,480
1987	05/06	S9/S12	2,342.19	−4.41%	$75,974
1987	06/22	B4	2,445.51	7.92%	$81,991
1987	10/01	S9	2,639.2	34.12%	$109,966
1987	10/19	B16	1,738.74	58.42%	$174,211
1989	10/03	S9	2,754.56	3.53%	$180,357
1989	10/16	B17	2,657.38	5.73%	$190,697
1990	01/03	S9	2,809.73	8.85%	$207,576
1990	01/25	B17	2,561.04	16.37%	$241,549
1990	07/13	S9	2,980.20	17.69%	$284,282
1990	9/24	B17	2,452.97	34.78%	$383,157
1992	04/14	S9	3,306.13	0.56%	$385,286
1992	06/17	B20	3,287.76	1.20%	$389,922
1992	09/15	S9	3,327.32	3.81%	$404,771
1992	10/02	B20	3,200.61	22.98%	$497,779
1994	10/19	S9	3,936.04	−0.94%	$493,098
1995	02/22	B10	3,973.05	33.52%	$658,405
1996	01/29	S9	5,304.98	−1.89%	$645,984
1996	02/01	B18	5,405.06	5.08%	$678,823
1996	08/02	S9	5,679.83	−2.79%	$659,857
1996	09/13	B10	5,838.52	14.82%	$757,648
1997	01/10	S9	6,703.79	−2.18%	$741,120
1997	01/22	B4	6,850.03	2.03%	$756,152
1997	02/14	S9	6,988.96	−0.17%	$754,861
1997	03/07	B18	7,000.89	−2.39%	$736,822
1997	04/22	S9	6,833.59	−5.57%	$695,752
1997	05/05	B4	7,214.49	11.10%	$772,999
1997	10/01	S12	8,015.50	6.45%	$822,876

(Continued)

TABLE 13.1 *(Continued)*

Date		Signals B=Buy S=Sell	Close	Percent Gain	$500 Investment Compounded
1997	10/28	B19	7,498.32	4.38% gain on long trade	$858,903
1997	11/20	S12	7,826.61	−5.99% gain on short sale	$807,434
1998	02/10	B4	8,295.61	10.22%	$889,935
1998	04/23	S9	9,143.23	14.86%	$1,022,166
1998	10/02	B17	7,784.69	17.98%	$1,205,937
1999	01/04	S9	9,184.27	10.33%	$1,330,474
2001	09/21	B16	8,235.81	23.81%	$1,647,306
2002	01/07	S12	10,197.04	−1.62%	$1,620,544
2002	04/01	B9	10,362.70	−1.15%	$1,601,931
2002	05/15	S12	10,243.68	20.04%	$1,922,889
2002	07/24	B19	8,191.29	7.11%	$2,059,578
2003	01/06	S9	8,773.57	14.24%	$2,352,898
2003	03/11	B17	7,524.06	40.09%	$3,305,667
2004	04/04	S9	10,558.37	5.49%	$3,487,290
2004	05/10	B20	9,990.02	2.89%	$3,588,079
2005	04/14	S10	10,278.75	0.59%	$3,609,076
2005	04/21	B19	10,218.60		
2005	09/30	Open	10,569		

Source: www.tigersoft.com.

The Peerless system has been similarly applied to the S&P 500, from 1970, and the results are equally impressive. Using these signals from May 27, 1970, through September 20, 2005 (seen in Table 13.2), would have seen a starting $500 compound to more than $1.7 million (assuming no withdrawals or additions, and no taxes paid); 85.7% of the Buys were profitable, with an average gain of approximately 13%; 78% of the Sells were profitable, each with an average gain of approximately 5.7%.

What is especially impressive is the large percentage of Sells that were profitable during a 35-year period when the S&P 500 advanced from an index level of 72.77 to 1159.95, almost a 15-fold increase, when this study was compiled on September 30, 2005.

TABLE 13.2 Peerless System Using the S&P 500 Since 1970

Date		Signals B=Buy S=Sell	Close	Percent Gain (on Next Reversing Signal)	$500 Investment Compounded
1970	05/27	B19	72.77	4.91%	$525
1970	07/16	S12	76.34	0.68%	$528
1970	08/11	B9	75.82	12.15%	$592
1970	11/11	S12	85.03	−5.45%	$560
1970	12/15	B4	89.66	11.52%	$625
1971	08/17	S12	99.99	6.00%	$662
1971	11/30	B12	93.99	16.55%	$772
1972	04/06	S9	109.55	3.25%	$797
1972	05/03	B20	105.99	0.66%	$802
1972	05/22	S12	106.69	0.81%	$808
1972	7/18	B20	105.83	4.35%	$844
1972	8/04	S12	110.43	2.65%	$866
1972	10/17	B20	107.5	11.23%	$963
1973	01/03	S9	119.57	9.63%	$1,056
1973	09/25	B4	108.05	3.08%	$1,088
1973	10/26	S9	111.38	16.23%	$1,265
1974	02/07	B9	93.3	0.48%	$1,271
1974	04/19	S9	93.75	30.72%	$1,662
1974	10/07	B19	64.95	33.76%	$2,229
1975	08/29	S12	86.88	−1.10%	$2,198
1975	12/04	B9	87.84	14.50%	$2,517
1976	03/09	S12	100.58	1.08%	$2,544
1976	05/25	B20	99.49	−2.73%	$2,475
1977	05/25	S10	96.77	4.07%	$2,576
1977	12/06	B9	92.83	−2.36%	$2,515
1978	01/09	S10	90.64	3.31%	$2,598
1978	02/23	B9	87.64	11.57%	$2,899
1978	07/17	S12	97.78	−5.86%	$2,729
1978	08/03	B4	103.51	0.92%	$2,754
1978	10/10	S12	104.46	7.29%	$2,955
1978	11/01	B19	96.85	14.06%	$3,370
1979	09/21	S9	110.47	5.96%	$3,571
1979	11/21	B9	103.89	6.89%	$3,817
1980	01/06	S12	111.05	9.34%	$4,173

(Continued)

TABLE 13.2   *(Continued)*

Date		Signals B=Buy S=Sell	Close	Percent Gain (on Next Reversing Signal)	$500 Investment Compounded
1980	03/28	B19	100.68	39.45%	$5,820
1980	11/20	S12	140.40	7/97%	$6,231
1980	12/09	B17	130.48	4.49%	$6,511
1981	01/02	S12	136.34	3.65%	$6,749
1981	01/21	B9	131.36	−1.16%	$6,670
1981	02/26	S9	129.84	11.02%	$7,406
1981	09/28	B19	115.53	−5.16%	$7,024
1982	07/12	S9	109.57	−0.48%	$7,058
1982	08/17	B12	109.04	33.14%	$9,397
1983	01/07	S12	145.18	3.59%	$9,734
1983	01/24	B9	139.97	17.33%	$11,421
1983	09/01	S9	164.23	−1.04%	$11,302
1984	01/24	B9	165.94	−3.03%	$10,959
1984	02/03	S10	160.91	3.37%	$11,329
1984	04/06	B20	155.48	3.99%	$11,781
1984	05/01	S12	161.68	3.65%	$12,211
1984	05/18	B20	155.78	19.64%	$14,609
1985	10/14	S9	186.37	−6.62%	$13,642
1985	11/18	B4	198.71	7.17%	$14,620
1986	02/05	S9	212.96	−1.54%	$14,395
1986	02/10	B4	216.24	12.81%	$16,239
1986	06/04	S9	243.94	0.46%	$16,313
1986	07/09	B9	242.82	0.21%	$16,348
1986	08/12	S9	243.34	3.35%	$16,896
1986	09/11	B17	235.18	27.74%	$21,583
1987	04/03	S9	300.41	5.32%	$22,730
1987	04/15	B19	284.44	3.88%	$23,611
1987	05/06	S12	295.47	−4.80%	$22,478
1987	06/22	B4	309.65	5.71%	$23,762
1987	10/01	S9	327.33	31.31%	$31,202
1987	10/19	B16	224.84	57.76%	$49,224
1989	10/03	S9	354.71	3.34%	$50,870
1989	10/16	B17	342.85	4.64%	$53,231
1990	01/03	S9	358.76	9.11%	$58,079

TABLE 13.2   *(Continued)*

Date		Signals B=Buy S=Sell	Close	Percent Gain (on Next Reversing Signal)	$500 Investment Compounded
1990	01/25	B17	326.08	12.64%	$65,423
1990	07/13	S9	367.31	17.08%	$76,594
1990	09/24	B17	304.59	35.39%	$103,702
1992	04/14	S9	412.39	2.46%	$106,250
1992	06/17	B20	402.26	4.35%	$110,875
1992	09/15	S9	419.77	2.22%	$113,331
1992	10/02	B20	410.47	14.57%	$129,845
1994	10/19	S9	470.28	−1.78%	$127,537
1995	02/03	B10	478.64	58.68%	$202,373
1997	01/10	S9	759.5	−3.52%	$195,254
1997	01/22	B4	786.22	−1.48%	$192,373
1997	04/22	S9	774.62	−7.19%	$178,545
1997	05/05	B4	830.3	15.07%	$205,444
1997	10/01	S12	955.39	3.57%	$212,788
1997	10/28	B19	921.24	23.58%	$262,966
1997	04/23	S9	1,138.48	11.94%	$294,351
1998	10/02	B17	1,002.6	22.49%	$360,555
1999	01/04	S12	1,228.1	−2.12%	$352,922
1999	10/18	B8	1,254.1	16.77%	$412,117
2000	03/17	S12	1,464.45	34.05%	$552,445
2001	09/21	B16	965.8	20.62%	$666,331
2002	01/07	S12	1,164.9	1.58%	$676,828
2002	04/01	B9	1,146.55	−4.84%	$644,065
2002	05/15	S12	1,091.05	22.69%	$790,227
2002	07/24	B19	843.45	10.14%	$870,379
2003	01/06	S9	929	13.81%	$990,536
2003	03/11	B17	800.75	43.38%	$1,420,274
2004	04/064	S9	1,148.15	5.32%	$1,495,794
2004	05/10	B20	1,087.10	10.58%	$1,654,028
2005	04/14	S8	1,202.10	3.51%	$1,712,024
2005	04/21	B19	1,159.95	Open as of 9/30/3005 with S&P 500 at 1,228.81	

Source: http://www.tigersoft.com/sp500/sp.500Results.htm for S&P 500.

If you elect to invest in the Peerless software, be patient. First, invest the time and energy to study and understand the signals. Bill is a ready and willing resource for technical support and academic dialogue.

Contact Information:
Dr. William Schmidt, Ph.D.
Tiger Software
P.O. Box 9491
San Diego, CA 92169
Phone: 858-273-5900
E-mail: william_schmidt@hotmail.com

WORDEN BROTHERS' TELECHART PLATINUM

I have been a Worden user since 1991, when the Tiger and Peerless software could be updated with Telechart data. I liked the Telechart service, so I stayed. I have gone through numerous upgraded versions since the company's first DOS-based system, and each upgrade has offered many valuable new features.

At its heart, *Telechart is a technical analysis graphics program, but it really is much more than that.* Sure, it is one of the slickest graphics packages around, but as a subscriber you also get the benefit of the TC2000 community of users. As a privately held concern, Worden does not disclose the number of subscribers for its different levels of service, or in aggregate, but the user numbers they are issuing today for new subscribers is well into six figures. Of course, many older subscribers will have decided that technical analysis or regular monitoring of charts is just not for them, but customer attrition is a substantial fact of life in any business. The important thing is that an increasing number of people are discovering the world of technical analysis through the Worden product, and many are eager to share ideas and refine investment and trading concepts.

Don Worden, the patriarch of the Worden family, is a recognized and practiced expert in technical analysis of both the overall market and individual stocks, having authored several books. His creative and insightful daily commentary alone is worth the price of admission, and he frequently shares the insights of users who e-mail him with notes and commentary. In fact, he encourages such notes by "knighting" subscribers who share comments where it is evident that they "think for themselves."

Telechart has three levels of service. The Wordens are so confident that you will find value in their software that they provide *free* access to their web site in level one, just by registering. You get access to all of the homepage articles, some video notes, discussion boards, and even free technical support via e-mail and telephone. If you are new to technical analysis, invest some time in exploring the web site content and commentary before deciding about the paid-for services. That way, should you decide to become a paid subscriber to one of the other services, you will have a much more satisfying and (presumably) profitable experience.

The *Telechart Gold* level of service costs $29.99 per month (discounts for 1-year and 2-year packages paid for in advance) and features Worden's award-winning graphics and technical analysis package. The magazine *Technical Analysis of Stocks and Commodities* has named it the "Best Stock Software Under $200" for 12 straight years, from 1993 to 2005, and the "Best End of Day Stock Data" from 1999 to 2005.

You can scan, analyze, sort, and manage tons of data with pre-set screens and watch lists, or customize your own. Stock splits and corrected data are managed for you, downloaded when you update your data (no extra charge). If you miss a day or two, don't worry. The next time you update everything will be brought up-to-date. Don and Peter Worden frequently attach notes to certain stocks, as can other users, and they attach charts with the indicators they are using to evaluate ideas. For those who like to see what kind of substance there might be behind their technically derived opportunities, Telechart offers some basic fundamental information (sales, earnings, growth rates, etc.), which you can access by just a touch of a button on the screen.

Telechart Platinum ($99.99 per month) adds streaming, real-time data to the mix. You can perform all of the technical analysis functions of the Gold service, and more, but on a real-time basis. Moreover, there are Clubs organized by users where ideas and methodologies are shared, as well as real-time chat that can be turned on for system-wide monitoring of ideas, or just focused on the banter in one or two clubs. This is where the idea of "community" reaches critical mass. Every single one of the Worden users represents somebody from which you might learn something, or use as a sounding board for a concept you are contemplating. Obviously, some are farther along in their market education than others, so you have to carefully pick and choose, and understand their time perspective. Are they making their decisions using monthly bar charts (very long-term), or five-minute candlestick charts (very short-term)? Telechart Platinum users range from professional hedge fund managers and registered investment advisors to neophytes.

But being new to the market doesn't make them stupid or their perspectives less valuable. There are many who have had success in other fields, and have turned to trading and investing in retirement as a second career. I've had exchanges with former engineers, mathematicians, college professors, neurosurgeons, and professional athletes. Each one brings a fresh perspective.

In the Telechart services, you can look at a wide array of broad stock market indexes, industry sectors, and just about any stock that is traded on a senior U.S. exchange (data for OTC Bulletin Board and Pink Sheets Stocks is not available). And the technical analysis constructs are broad in number and as easy and intuitive to use as anyone could hope for.

As this book went to press, Worden is introducing a completely new software platform that seamlessly integrates with Telechart 2007. The new product is called SnapSheet, built on patent-pending block technology.

Contact Information:

Go to www.wataugamgt.com and click on TCNet hyperlink, which will direct you to the Worden web site. They like to track where interest in their services comes from, and your accessing their site from the Watauga site facilitates this mission, letting them know it is coming from this book or someone browsing the Watauga Equity Management web site.

THETA RESEARCH

If you are looking for a money manager that actively employs market timing methodologies, Theta Research is a good place to start. It is a completely independent, performance analytics firm that continuously monitors about 450 timing and allocation models of approximately 150 registered investment advisors. Located on the Internet at www.thetaresearch.com, the firm has three levels of service: *individual, professional, and corporate.*

On a daily basis, the service compiles data on each of the management models it monitors. Some of the models, like those of my firm (Watauga Equity Management), make relatively few allocations during an average year. Others are quite active. Some use Rydex funds; others use ProFunds. I am not aware of any Direxionfunds-based models, yet, on the Theta site.

The Theta service provides access to daily rankings, charts of performance (updated daily), access to various performance statistics (like R-Squared and Correlation), and manager contact information. The screen print in Figure 13.3 is from the home page at www.thetaresearch.com.

Once inside the service, you can create data filters, and sort data by any one of a number of selection criteria. Build and analyze a "manager of

Quick Stats from our Database					
	Best Performing Theta Model	S&P 500	Dow 30	OTC 100	Nasdaq Comp
QTD	20.70%	-1.14%	1.52%	-5.71%	-5.53%
YTD	32.62%	2.55%	5.24%	-2.36%	0.23%
3 Month	38.35%	-0.72%	1.96%	-4.18%	-3.35%
6 Month	33.97%	0.94%	3.17%	-5.57%	-2.33%
12 Month	59.71%	6.89%	7.03%	3.72%	6.72%
24 Month	120.50%	14.82%	11.56%	10.49%	11.85%
36 Month	110.12%	37.18%	31.13%	42.15%	46.37%
48 Month	153.89%	18.12%	11.62%	28.20%	33.04%
60 Month	99.23%	0.18%	2.48%	-18.07%	-1.81%

Data above is as of market close 05/26/2006. Index calculations are derived from index values published by Standard and Poors, Dow Inc., and the NASDAQ and do not include reinvested dividends.

Subscriptions are available for as little as 60¢ per market day (paid Annually)

Subscribe Now

Subscription Feature Comparison			
Feature	Individual	Professional	Corporate
Daily Access to Manager Rankings	✓	✓	✓
Daily Access to Charts	✓	✓	✓
Daily Access to Statistics	✓	✓	✓
Daily Access To Manager Information	✓	✓	✓
Create Custom Data Filters	✓	✓	✓
Ability to Sort Data on Many Criteria	✓	✓	✓
Create Favorites List For Quick Viewing	✓	✓	✓
Download Data for further analysis [1]	✓	✓	✓
Manager Monitoring - Email Notification of Performance and Risk		✓	✓
Correlation Studies		✓	✓
Build and Analyze Manager of Manager Portfolios		✓	✓
Create Viewable Lists for Reps			✓
Monthly Billing for Data Downloads			✓

FIGURE 13.3   Theta Research Home Page

Source: Copyright © 2006 Theta Investment Research, LLC.

managers" portfolio. Set up for e-mail notifications of certain performance and risk criteria.

One particularly interesting feature programmed into Theta's subscriber service is an ability to graphically compare selected models against several selected benchmarks, including the S&P 500, S&P 1500, NASDAQ 100, NASDAQ Composite, Vanguard Long Term Bond Fund, and a 60% Equity/40% Long Term Bond Allocation.

For example, I ran Watauga Equity Management's Active Index service against the S&P 1500 for the past 36 months (you can also look at 3-month, 6-month, 12-month, 24-month, 48-month, and 60-month periods if there is sufficient data), because smaller-capitalization stocks have been relatively good performers. (See Figure 13.4.)

Despite a timing miscue in early 2005, *Active Index* is still outperforming the S&P 1500 by a pretty wide margin over the past 36 months.

As can be seen in Figures 13.5 and 13.6, our *Active Index* performance advantage expands considerably when you begin to put the Bond component into the comparison picture.

Over 36 months, there is a big divide between the performance gained by Watauga Equity Management's *Active Index* versus the Vanguard Long Term Bond Fund.

FIGURE 13.4 Theta Research Comparison, *Active Index* versus S&P 500 Benchmark

Source: Copyright © 2006 Theta Investment Research, LLC.

FIGURE 13.5   Theta Research Comparison, *Active Index* versus 60% Equity/40% Bond Allocation

Source: Copyright © 2006 Theta Investment Research, LLC.

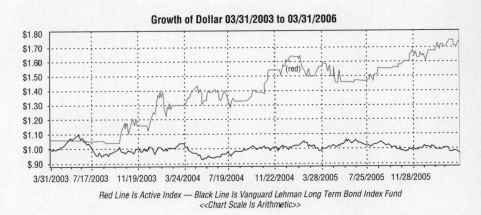

FIGURE 13.6   Theta Research Comparison Chart: *Active Index* versus Vanguard Long-Term Bond Fund

Source: Copyright © 2006 Theta Investment Research, LLC.

By the way, since we made a big deal about R-Squared in Chapter 1, Theta Research calculates Active Index's R-Squared versus the S&P 500 to be 24%. So even though the overall market is our trading vehicle, we have a significantly higher compounded rate of return (21%) than the S&P 500 (10%) over the past 36 months, and the overall market only explains 24% of performance. That means that approximately 76% of the performance is explained by what the manager (Watauga Equity Management) is doing.

Contact Information:

Theta Investment Research LLC
518 Kimberton Road, Suite 404
Phoenixville, PA 19460
Phone: 610-495-0180
Fax: 610-495-0930
E-mail: info@thetaresearch.com

This is a very robust service. There are many tools here, but some other screen shots from www.thetaresearch.com are located in Figure 13.7.

All of the Theta-monitored management models are real money, not hypothetical. Performance analysis for one management model monitored by Theta is shown in Figure 13.8.

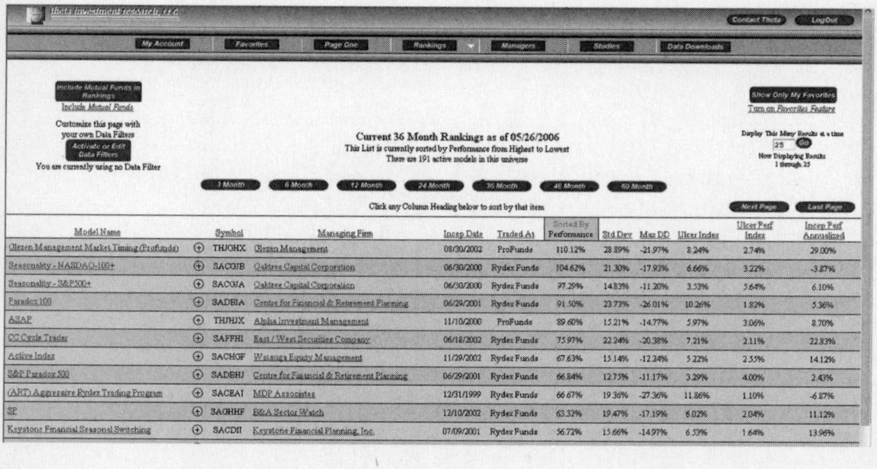

Model Name	Symbol	Managing Firm	Incep Date	Traded At	Sorted By Performance	Std Dev	Max DD	Ulcer Index	Ulcer Perf Index	Incep Perf Annualized
Glezen Management Market Timing (Profunds)	THJOHX	Glezen Management	08/30/2002	ProFunds	110.12%	28.89%	-21.97%	8.24%	2.74%	29.00%
Seasonality - NASDAQ-100+	SACGJB	Oaktree Capital Corporation	06/30/2000	Rydex Funds	104.62%	21.30%	-17.93%	6.66%	3.22%	-3.87%
Seasonality - S&P500+	SACGJA	Oaktree Capital Corporation	06/30/2000	Rydex Funds	97.29%	14.83%	-11.20%	3.53%	5.64%	6.10%
Paradox 100	SADBIA	Centre for Financial & Retirement Planning	06/29/2001	Rydex Funds	91.50%	23.73%	-26.01%	10.26%	1.82%	5.36%
ASAP	THJHJX	Alpha Investment Management	11/10/2000	ProFunds	89.60%	15.21%	-14.77%	5.97%	3.06%	8.70%
CC Cycle Trader	SAFFHI	East / West Securities Company	06/18/2002	Rydex Funds	75.97%	22.24%	-20.38%	7.21%	2.11%	22.83%
Active Index	SACHGF	Watauga Equity Management	11/29/2002	Rydex Funds	67.63%	15.14%	-12.24%	5.22%	2.55%	14.12%
S&P Paradox 500	SADBHJ	Centre for Financial & Retirement Planning	06/29/2001	Rydex Funds	66.84%	12.75%	-11.17%	3.29%	4.00%	2.43%
(ART) Aggressive Rydex Trading Program	SACEAI	MDP Associates	12/31/1999	Rydex Funds	66.67%	19.36%	-27.36%	11.86%	1.10%	-6.87%
SP	SAGHHF	B&A Sector Watch	12/10/2002	Rydex Funds	63.32%	19.47%	-17.19%	6.02%	2.04%	11.12%
Keystone Financial Seasonal Switching	SACDII	Keystone Financial Planning, Inc.	07/09/2001	Rydex Funds	56.72%	15.66%	-14.97%	6.53%	1.64%	13.96%

FIGURE 13.7 Theta Research Screen Shots
Source: Copyright © 2006 Theta Investment Research, LLC

Performance and Risk Statistics As of 05/26/2006											
Stat	3M	6M	12M	24M	36M	48M	60M	QTD	YTD	Incep	Incep/Ann
Perf	3.52%	5.79%	21.93%	28.61%	67.63%	N/A	N/A	0.64%	10.72%	58.59%	14.12%
StdDev (Annualized)	19.68%	17.77%	8.24%	13.09%	15.14%	N/A	N/A	--	--	17.94%	--
Max DD	-6.01%	-6.01%	-6.01%	-12.24%	-12.24%	N/A	N/A	-6.01%	-6.01%	-25.37%	--
Ulcer Index	2.00%	1.87%	1.36%	5.65%	5.22%	N/A	N/A	--	--	7.88%	--
Ulcer Perf Index	4.73%	3.51%	12.11%	1.42%	2.55%	N/A	N/A	--	--	1.11%	--

Percentile Ranking Statistics As of 05/26/2006					
Period	Perf Rank	MaxDD Rank	STD Rank	UI Rank	UPI Rank
3 Month	80th	43rd	58th	67th	79th
6 Month	79th	51st	65th	77th	80th
12 Month	90th	64th	75th	89th	98th
24 Month	84th	46th	51st	49th	76th
36 Month	88th	39th	73rd	71st	86th
48 Month	--	--	--	--	--
60 Month	--	--	--	--	--

FIGURE 13.8 Theta Research Performance Analysis

Source: Copyright © 2006 Theta Investment Research, LLC.

TRADERDOC.COM

A market is a market is a market. I alluded to this previously when I suggested that a good technical analysis tool, or at least the strategies used to make trading decisions, have a degree of universality to them. They work in pork bellies or individual stocks, in cotton futures or the overall stock market.

I have a hard time embracing trend-following-derived methods, because they conflict with my contrarian personality. Nonetheless, I am open-minded and last year succumbed to a natural curiosity. Dr. Charles Schaap and his wife, Candy, are the architects of methodologies that are, at their core, trend-following, but have a logical sense and an implementation elegance that is irresistible. And once you master the conceptual and strategic basics, just about anyone can put them to work, in any trading or investing time period, in any type of market vehicle.

TraderDoc has expanded on technical indicators first developed by J. Welles Wilder a quarter-century ago, the ADX (Average Directional Movement Index) and DMI (Directional Movement Indicator). The technical methods that he advances are based solely on price and its trends. Price is the ultimate arbiter of value. His focus, in fact, is on what he calls "power trends."

Combining TraderDoc's trading strategies with the sorting, screening, and graphing capabilities of *TCNet* or *Telechart Platinum* is powerful. I'm not going to give away his work, but I suggest that anyone seriously interested in learning about a disciplined approach to investing in stocks or the overall market take a look at the Schaaps' work. In early 2006, he self-published a book, *ADXcellence: Power Trend Strategies* ($149), that may be the most definitive work ever published on approaches using ADX, DMI, and another interesting technical construct, "pivots," which I first saw many years ago being used by commodity traders on the floor of the Chicago Mercantile Exchange and the Chicago Board of Trade.

In Dr. Schaap's words, "ADXcellence tells us when to get in a trade and when to stay out. It keeps us on the right side of trend direction and keeps us trading with the strongest trends. Following the principles and strategies in this book will reduce the stress of trading decisions and improve results."

At $149, the book is designed for serious traders. You can order it by visiting the www.stockmarketstore.com web site.

SCHREINER CAPITAL MANAGEMENT

With an estimated $115 million under management and in business since 1989, Schreiner Capital Management (SCM) is one of the pioneers in active asset allocation strategies. SCM offers five different management models, three focused on sectors and two on the NASDAQ 100 Index. The sector models use Fidelity's sector funds, while the NASDAQ 100 models use Rydex funds. Founder and lead manager Roger Schreiner is a student of the market, and an enthusiastic advocate of active asset allocation practices for return enhancement and better risk management. Theta Research was originally a subsidiary of Schreiner Capital Management.

SCM has been around a lot longer than most active allocation managers and is making a deliberate effort to earn premium compensation.

Contact Information:

Schreiner Capital Management
111 Summit Drive, Suite 100
Exton, PA 19341
Phone: 800-351-0268
E-mail: info@scminvest.com
Web site: www.selectadvisor.com

Afterword

The capital markets for publicly owned companies are the energy of capitalism. People invent things and build companies around their inventions. Entrepreneurs build factories and office buildings, conduct research and development, and spend money on a multitude of essential corporate activities. They need capital to make these things happen. And, to do these things on any kind of size or scale *the public capital markets are necessary to facilitate and satisfy those financing needs.*

Of course, it is a two-way street. The investors providing capital to meet these needs may be pension funds, insurance companies, banks, foundations, mutual funds, or individuals. Whatever the source, the public stock market is important because it provides investors with a source of ready liquidity for their investments—and investment returns. Companies pay dividends to shareholders as a way of returning profits *and* the publicly traded markets are an easy, liquid way for investors to realize appreciation in the value of their stock ownership, as other investors recognize the business opportunities being pursued and capitalized on by these companies.

I believe steadfastly in the fidelity and persistence of capitalism and market-driven economies, at once for the *efficiencies* that provide stability and predictability to the marketplace, as well as for the market *inefficiencies* that provide opportunities for extraordinary reward to the insightful, the resourceful, and the responsive.

Throughout this book, I have discussed how the financial services industry oversold the concept and practice of diversification in the last 30 years. It is probably more an act of self-preservation, since the brokerage community has been forced increasingly to asset-based fee compensation as they watched full service commissions for trade execution evaporate with the commoditization of buying and selling securities. Open markets where there is no special intellectual property engender such price competition.

I find it ironic that the very asset that *could* have commanded premium compensation from trade execution—research—has been largely abandoned, or at least deemphasized by the greater brokerage community. *Maybe they realized that conventional equity research models, as practiced, were adding little value to investors—the same conclusion I reached, in frustration, more than 25 years ago when the firms' research department ideas I was peddling as a broker were so much worthless reams of paper, for the most part.*

Research that helps investors earn profitable results in the aftermarket— that is, from trading that occurs on the exchanges and over-the-counter markets after companies go public—is a very different animal from *corporate finance-related equity research*. While there are elements of value that overlap between the two activities, aftermarket research needs to also take into consideration the psychological aspects of investor expectations, especially valuation concepts related to fear and greed.

To review some concepts discussed earlier, there are three primary influences to equity investment performance:

1. Activities at the individual company level
2. Activities in the industry sector in which a company operates
3. Activities with the overall stock market

If you only own one stock, the greater explanation of performance is likely to come from company-level and industry-level factors. The more diversified the portfolio, the greater the importance of overall market direction. It's as simple as that.

I made a case that the financial services industry oversold the concept of diversification in the last 30 years. Consequently, so many of the returns from traditional equity portfolios are mediocre, rather than superior. If you are going to be a traditional type of active investor or manager and earn superior returns, then you must truly become a better stock picker—or put the power of the overall stock market to work for you, and not become its victim.

Don't be a *closet indexer*. Don't be *average*. Don't be mediocre. Make your stock investments mean something, either concentrating assets in fewer stocks that you know have superior outlooks, or focusing on the industry sectors that you feel are going to be the next big performers.

Diversify your assets in several stocks *operating in those few sectors*.

Be like Fidelity's William Danoff or CGM's Ken Heebner who, as I pointed out in Chapter 1, mostly achieve higher alpha (and lower R-Squared) by being right about their industry concentrations. Use your research skills to develop an investment thesis that you can adopt with conviction, then put your money behind your conviction. That's what the active portfolio managers deserving of premium compensation do.

Once in a while, you will hit a sour note. You'll be wrong, or you'll be early, or you'll be late. Traditional managers must be willing to *earn* premium fee compensation if they are to continue competing effectively. Closet indexers advertising themselves as active managers are being discovered as frauds undeserving of premium fee compensation. They are being called out of the closet.

The financial markets are dynamic, arguably more volatile today than at any other time in history. In today's world of rapid technology obsolescence, fast-changing business models, and a more favorable tax environment, superior returns are earned not by buying and holding individual equities through long cycles, but by recognizing when high valuations are *probably* unsustainable—and reallocating capital to other, better-valued ideas *and* pursuing strategies that take advantage of the overall market's importance to portfolio performance. Indeed, active management is an important key that can open the door of above-average returns and better risk management.

So you are sold on diversification. That's okay, because you still don't have to be satisfied with mediocrity. You can earn superior returns and still maintain a highly diversified discipline by *moving away from merely indexing* and *toward alternative investing*. In order to compete effectively, you must *use* the overall market. You must take advantage of the new investment and trading products, to neutralize the impact of corrective or declining markets. *You must put the number-1 factor in the performance of any well-diversified portfolio—the Market—to work for you, rather than allow yourself to become its victim.*

In a well-thought article on his web site, www.dowtheoryletters.com, Richard Russell advances, "All investing and speculation is basically an exercise in attempting to beat time." Trying to pick a winning stock, trying to sell out at the top, trying to apportion investment capital over several asset classes, trying to earn profits through in-and-out trading, selling covered call options, buying put options—these are all attempts to beat time or to use time to beat itself, Russell asserts.

Indeed, *time* is the very essence of timing, and *the success of every investment or trading decision we make is dependent on timing.* In fact, timing is the third dimension of risk, along with concentration and leverage.

Buy low. Sell high. Earn profits. For heaven's sake, don't be a hypocrite and decry timing when that is part and parcel of what every single investor or trader is doing: making a timing decision, whether he realizes or not. The timing element is critical to investment results, whether the investor is passive or active.

An investor who bought Ceradyne (NASDAQ: CRDN) in June 2003, at a split-adjusted price of $6.85 and still holds the stock today near $54 is a fortunate soul. His timing was good.

The investor who bought Ceradyne seven years earlier, at $4.67, but got scared and liquidated his position when the stock declined to $1.36 less than three years later, was not so lucky. His timing was bad.

An investor bought General Motors (NYSE: GM) in September 1987, right at the top of the market before the Crash, near $38. He held the stock through some anxious times over the next five years, seeing GM share prices not once, not twice, not three times, but *four times* get their value cut almost in half after recovering to break even near $38. Finally, in May 2000, he senses the market is frothy and fears growing competition from the likes of Toyota, BMW, and Subaru. So he sells, picking off what turns out to be the top of the market, with GM shares at $94. For his nearly 13 years' patience in riding GM "through thick and thin," and then his good timing at selling out near the top, he was rewarded with a compounded rate of return of about 7.2%.

That's a rather paltry, mediocre investment return considering the risk he undertook, but superior to the poor guy who waited eight years before investing, buying GM right near the last correction bottom before the big run-up, in early 1995, at $31. His broker told him to "buy and hold" it. Put it away in your safety deposit box. It pays a great dividend, and they increase the dividend as the years go by. When the stock reached $94, he was the master of his universe and the toast of every cocktail party for his apparently good timing.

About 11 years after his investment, in late 2005, GM was trading at under $24. Nearly a 25% loss was his reward for being patient. Today, as I write this, it has recovered to $28. His timing is still rotten because so far the compounded rate of return on his investment over the 11 years of his hold is negative!

Ibbotson & Associates calculated that the nominal return for the S&P

500 between 1926 and 2004 averaged 10.43%, including reinvestment of dividends; $1 grew to about $2,531, at this rate.

But Thornburg Investment Management, an advisory firm based in Santa Fe, New Mexico, suggests that the real, *real* rate of return on an investment must account for taxes on the dividends, the price of inflation, and expenses (commissions, management fees, etc.). Taking those factors into account, Thornburg says on its web site, www.thornburg investments.com, *the real, real rate of return for the S&P from 1926 to 2004 was just 4.96%*. And that doesn't even account for any capital gains taxes that might have to have been paid when the Standard & Poor's investment committee forces you to sell one stock out of its index and replace it with another!

By the way, *this latter thought isn't frivolous.* If you own mutual funds, even index funds, you're well aware that you get a tax document every year from your mutual fund company that tells how much was distributed to you the previous year in dividends and capital gains distributions. These are taxable if you don't hold your funds in a tax-qualified plan.

We're all trying to beat time, Russell says. Let's take a guy 54 years old. We'll assume that he has 20 more good earning years left. He has $50,000 in retirement savings, and figures that he can put away an additional $5,000 per year (10% of his gross annual earnings), on average, given his current spending profile and earnings level. Taking into account inflation, he guestimates a need for about $1 million in the bank at the end of 20 years to pay for living and noncatastrophic medical expenses for the rest of his life.

With that amount of initial principal in savings, that much time, and that level of additional investment every year, he needs to earn an annual compounded rate of return of just under 14.1% in a tax-deferred account. *He needs a superior return. If he settles for mediocre*, say an 8% compounded rate of return that might be reasonable to expect from the S&P 500 over the next 20 years, *his money doesn't get the job done*. He would only have a little more than $480,000, *or not quite half of his targeted need.*

As investors we demand more and we expect more from our investment capital. An enlightened populace has been taught by the financial services industry about the virtues of stock market investing as a wealth accumulation vehicle. *But that same group is smart enough to become further enlightened, too.*

These New Age investors will not stand by and let money managers and asset allocation professionals get rich on providing them, the investors taking the financial risks, with simply mediocre returns. *They will demand superior returns and they will demand better management of risk* than is currently being provided. *Neither of those objectives is satisfied by traditional, long-only asset management methods*, nor by what have become commonly accepted (passive) asset allocation principles.

We want superior returns with less risk. And we can have both if we only think conceptually, and put the most important factors in investment performance to work *for* us, rather than allow ourselves to be their victim.

I am writing my concluding thoughts in this Afterword on March 10, 2006. Over the last three years since Theta Research began independently monitoring *my mutual fund asset allocation services, offered under the banner of Watauga Equity Management, my Index Plus (moderate risk) program has been fully invested in money market more than 53% of the time.* Even so, the *average annual compounded rate of return over that 36-month period is 15.10%.* Whether that is superior or not is up to individual judgment and perspective, but it is well above average—*and even out of the market, unexposed to risk, more often than in the market.*

Over the same 36 months ending March 10, 2006, according to Theta Research, my more aggressive Active Index program has been in 100% money market almost 40% of the time, but *through timing* has managed an *average annual compounded rate of return during that 36 months of more than 24.5%.* Our *average* annual return (the way most mutual funds calculate and sell their performance) is over 31%.

Do I have all the answers? No. Are we the best? Not by any stretch of the imagination.

But we are part of the new breed of investor/manager who is putting the overall market to work to fashion higher, more consistent investment returns, even with better management of risk.

As a result, in the months and years ahead we will be more effectively competing against the more established, traditional investors. If you are one of those traditional managers, there's no need to look over your shoulder. *Just know that we are coming.*

Index